ALSO BY MELISSA CLARK

THE FINER THINGS: CAVIAR AND CHAMPAGNE

THE *VEGETARIAN TIMES* MEDITERRANEAN COOKBOOK

SYLVIA'S SOUL FOOD FAMILY COOKBOOK

THE ICE CREAM MACHINE COOKBOOK

PASTA: COMFORT FOOD

THE SWEET BREAD MACHINE COOKBOOK

A KITCHEN PRIMER

THE INSTANT GOURMET

THE BOOK OF COFFEE

THE BREAD MACHINE COOKBOOK

The

NANTUCKET
RESTAURANTS

Cookbook

The
NANTUCKET
RESTAURANTS

Cookbook

MENUS AND RECIPES FROM THE FARAWAY ISLE

Melissa Clark and
Samara Farber Mormar

Photography by Cary Hazlegrove

VILLARD / NEW YORK

VILLARD BOOKS and colophon are registered trademarks of Random House, Inc.

Library of Congress Cataloging-in-Publication Data is available.

Printed in the United States of America on acid-free paper
Villard Books website address: www.villard.com

4 6 8 9 7 5 3

Book design by Caroline Cunningham

To the men In our lives—Paul, Mark, and Max

NANTUCKET

"Just a sandy wind-swept island"
What more would you have it be,
With a turquoise sky above it,
Around it a sapphire sea?

When its dawns are pearl and opal,
Its moons are crystal clear,
And its sunsets shower down gold dust
Till the diamond stars appear.

When to those who are born on the island,
And to many from over the sea
'Tis fairer than all its jewels
What more does it need to be?

By Mary E. Starbuck

1890s

PREFACE

My love affair with Nantucket began the very day I first set foot on its shores, in 1987. Friends from my small New Hampshire college suggested that Nantucket was *the* place to spend the summer, beaching it by day and earning big tips waiting tables by night. This quirky island and its small-town ways were all so strange to me at first. Lightship basket purses, "woodies," Nantucket Reds, clambakes, shopping at the dump and the thrift shop, widow's walks, ties covered with ducks, pants covered with whales, gray-shingled houses . . .

But I was quickly seduced by the sunsets that turn everything pink. I fell in love with being able to walk for miles and miles along the beaches without seeing another soul if I timed it right. Wild blueberries on the side of the road; a farm truck on Main Street; kids who really sell lemonade; a Fourth of July celebration complete with a watermelon-eating contest and fireworks on the beach; wildflowers bathed in a moody fog that rolls in as if on cue, curling your hair and sending you searching for a cozy cotton sweater to throw on over your August tan—for residents of Nantucket, these are daily realities, as they are now for my family and me.

Ironically, Nantucket, with its small-town feel, is where I became fascinated with gourmet food and fine dining, the sort normally associated with big cities. Here, we have dozens of restaurants to choose from that house world-class chefs with trend-setting creativity. Considering myself a fantastic waitress at the age of nineteen, I of course fully expected to land a job in one of them, but the truth of the matter is that I didn't know my arugula from my endive, or even my merlot from my sauvignon blanc.

Of all of the fine restaurants at the time, it was the Boarding House that I most wanted to be a part of. It was small and chic, a place where the beautiful people hung out and the serious food made way for some

even more serious partying once the kitchen closed. But the waiters there were way out of my league. Professional, seasoned (in other words, snobs, every one), not a college student among them. A friend of a friend got me in the door, and I think they took pity on me. They lured me into a job in the kitchen with the possibility of a few lunch shifts waiting tables later in the season. Of course I knew nothing about food and even less about what I was getting myself into. But by the end of the summer, not only did I know my arugula from my endive, but I knew my mâche, lollo rosso, oak leaf, and frisée as well. I grew to love the artistry and camaraderie of the kitchen. That was the beginning of a career in food that eventually took me back to New York City.

Eight years later my husband, Mark, came along and quite literally rescued me, offering me the possibility to choose to live just about anywhere in the world. I chose Nantucket, of course. We now live here year-round, along with our son, Max.

On the very first morning that I could once again call Nantucket home, I had an epiphany. There were so many restaurants I looked forward to eating in, it occurred to me that it would take weeks to visit them all. Per capita, Nantucket Island must have more fantastic food than just about anywhere else in the country, if not the world! Perhaps a cookbook was in the making! I made a list of restaurants on the back of an envelope. To qualify, a restaurant had to be well established, owner-operated, preferably even chef-owned, with innovative, original food and recipes worth sharing. The list grew from ten to eighteen. All of a sudden I thought I was really on to something. If I was so eager to try the island's wonderful fare, perhaps others not lucky enough to live here would want to read about the restaurants and re-create their recipes at home. I decided to call a friend and run it by her to see if I was crazy or if this might actually be a good idea. Whenever I have any food-related quandary, I call my friend the cookbook author and *New York Times* food columnist Melissa Clark.

Without Melissa's partnership, *The Nantucket Restaurants Cookbook* would be nothing but a good idea. She believed in this book from the beginning and agreed to put her name on the project and author it with me. Melissa took it to her agent, Janis Donnaud, who paired us with the perfect editor, Pamela Cannon at Villard, who brought our idea to print. Melissa is the brilliant writer and professional recipe maven who did an awful lot of the work, making me look good. She had some help too, of course, and is grateful to Sara Epstein, Amy Reiff, and Zoe Singer for their tireless work inputting, editing, and testing recipes.

Once Melissa had agreed to co-author the book and we worked out some of the mechanics, it was time to turn our thoughts to the visuals. The first time I saw Cary Hazlegrove's photography of Nantucket was, along with countless others, at the slide show she produces here each year. Her photographs of the island are so ethereal that they get inside you and become memories of your own. It is her daisy fields that I see more clearly now than one I have actually been to. Cary has a spirit and energy like no other person I've met, and I think it comes through in the beautiful images that she shares with us here. Even Cary needs a little help sometimes, and she found it in the capable hands of Macy Cassin and Alison Fader-Brock.

My favorite part of putting this book together was getting to work in the kitchens (while pregnant with Max!) with each of the talented chefs and restaurateurs profiled here. Not only did they agree to give up a day or more of their valuable time, during the busy summer season, but they did it with a warmth and excitement for the book that never ceased to amaze me. You'll find their names in the pages that follow. They are each deserving of a book all their own and I only hope that we have done them justice here.

To help ensure that we have, we invited the wise and wonderful Sarah Leah Chase to take a look, lend us some of her insight, and be a part of this labor of love by gracing us with her words of introduction. Her many suggestions and the delightful piece that follows have added much to the ability of this book to paint just the right picture and transport you into the dining rooms of these eighteen special restaurants.

There are, unfortunately, many deserving restaurants that we weren't able to include here for any number of reasons. *The Nantucket Restaurants Cookbook* is a sampling of many of the most unique gems that are found here. Apologies for not being able to feature every single one. We encourage all our readers to visit Nantucket and experience the wonderful restaurant scene for themselves.

—Samara Farber Mormar

CONTENTS

was so enraged he grabbed a big club and waded out through the sea to Nantucket, where he found his children's bones underneath a huge oak tree. Certainly not the sort of feasting we associate with the faraway island today!

The next well-known Nantucket eating story is even less cheery. We'd all love to imagine that the eighteenth- and nineteenth-century whalers who set off from Nantucket on worldly travels in search of sperm oil indulged in exotic cuisine in foreign ports of call, as we world travelers naturally do today. But Galápagos turtle was about the most unusual fare aboard ship, with a steady and dreadful diet of hardtack and water being much more the norm for the common sailor. And then there is the horrific story of the Nantucket whaling ship *Essex,* its shipwreck in 1820 in the vast Pacific Ocean, and the eventual cannibalism resorted to by its survivors. Not a very auspicious or engaging beginning to the history of fabulous eating surrounding Nantucket!

No, for that we need to turn to fiction and Herman Melville's epic mid-nineteenth-century masterpiece *Moby-Dick.* Chapter 15 is entitled "Chowder," and lo and behold it profiles a Nantucket restaurant called the Try Pots, an unusual choice of subject matter for a novel of this time period. The chapter reads not unlike one that you would find Samara Farber Mormar and Melissa Clark featuring in the following pages. The restaurant is described by

Melville as the "fishiest of all fishy places," and well deserving of its name, "for the pots there were always boiling chowders. Chowder for breakfast, and chowder for dinner, and chowder for supper, till you began to look for fish-bones coming through your clothes." The chowder itself is described with accolades akin to those diners today might apply to the Club Car's crabcakes or the Pearl's osetra scallops. Melville wrote: "But when that smoking chowder came in, the mystery was delightfully explained. . . . It was made of small juicy clams, scarcely bigger than hazel nuts [*sic*], mixed with pounded ship biscuit, and salted pork cut up into little flakes; the whole enriched with butter, and plentifully seasoned with pepper and salt. . . . the chowder being surpassingly excellent, we despatched it with great expedition."

For nearly the next hundred years the food cooked on Nantucket remained in the tradition of the Try Pots, following the Yankee way of making do with that which was on hand or economical. Then in 1946, Gwen and Harold Gaillard opened the Opera House Restaurant and Bar in town on South Water Street and the seed was firmly planted for the lively and eclectic restaurant scene that still flourishes on Nantucket more than fifty years later.

Back in 1946, Gwen recalls, there were only a few restaurants, "such as the lady at One Pleasant Street or Cy's Green Coffee Pot serving plain old Nantucket food." She and Harold wanted to bring the glamour

INTRODUCTION

These days it's easy to pick up any number of fashionable food or travel magazines and find a glossy spread on some superlative aspect of Nantucket Island. What makes Nantucket so in demand has much to do with what Nantucket once was, though properly weathered shingles, faded red pants, and rose-covered roofs are of more concern to most current lovers of this island than intimate knowledge of its fascinating past. Indeed, who has the time or inclination to be squirreled away in a musty museum corner poring over frail and worn whaling journals when miles of pristine beaches, compelling people, and stellar restaurants beckon at nearly every beautiful bend?

Nantucket is perhaps best seen as a place both haunted and enlivened by its past. Those who now live in its many old sea captains' houses must learn to make peace with the smattering of benign spirits who linger in creaky attics, while credible ghost stories abound, often recorded in local books or shared during riveting walking tours. Soon, it becomes logical to believe that some element or key to Nantucket's extraordinary restaurant scene of today must be rooted in the past. As a matter of fact, argument could be made that the human history of Nantucket Island began with eating, though not the sort of eating we Zagat-obsessed restaurant-goers dwell on today.

The island's first inhabitants were Indians, and it was they who named it *Nantucket*, meaning "the faraway island." The Indians also passed down the legend of its discovery in their tale of a great man-eating bird that supposedly lived on Nantucket. One day, as the story goes, the bird flew to the Cape Cod mainland in search of prey and seized the two children of a giant named Maushope. The bird then flew back to the island with the children and ate them. Maushope

and good food of restaurants they frequented in both New York and Europe to Nantucket. They hired a French chef and filled the dining and drinking spaces with folksy antiques, theater posters, and a piano. Gwen says she named the restaurant the Opera House simply because there was no reason not to.

When I first arrived on Nantucket in the summer of 1970, the Opera House had the grandest of reputations. I was thirteen and I lived with my aunt and uncle, who dined there many nights of the week, always returning home with endless raves over the fabulous food, peppered with outrageous tales of social interactions among the wealthy, notorious, and occasionally derelict clientele. I was so in awe of the place that I actually feared walking directly in front of it and would cross South Water Street to walk instead in front of Hardy's, a hardware store. I would sneak furtive glances across the street between the lush hanging baskets

of fuchsia that always adorned the restaurant's patio.

A few years later, I began to be treated to lunches and dinners at the Opera House, and it was always love at every inspired bite. The scene and ambience were every bit as delectable as the food, creating an impression of Paris in the 1920s rather than of a provincial Yankee outpost in the 1970s. Almost thirty years later, I now know that the combination of summering on Nantucket, eating at the Opera House, and cooking at home utilizing the island's garden and ocean largesse changed the course of my life for the culinary better, just as it has for so many of the restaurant proprietors and chefs profiled in this book: Chick Walsh at 21 Federal, Pat Tyler at the West Creek Café, Tom Proch at the Club Car, and more. Then there are the people who have worked in these establishments and in turn gone on to meld a little bit of the legacy with fresh energy in new restaurant ventures. The Nantucket restaurant community continues to grow like a Bartlett Farm tomato ripening under the August sun, intensifying rather than diluting.

Undoubtedly, Nantucket's bounty of superior ingredients from local, salt-misted farms and the surrounding waters has contributed to the success of its acclaimed restaurants, but there has to be more to it. Special people run these restaurants, many special and uncommonly appreciative people eat in

them, and all of it transpires on a very special island. My theory on why and how is twofold. First, I believe the islanders and many of the longtime visitors have developed via osmosis from our whaling ancestors—or, if you will, from their lingering spirits—a yin-yang love of worldly wanderlust countered by the feeling that only Nantucket can truly be considered home. Once one has seen and tasted the world, a bowl of island chowder is always comforting, yet we also crave the broader, trendier tastes piqued on our travels. And Nantucket restaurants and restaurateurs can deliver just that diversity in well over a dozen top-notch venues. Without conflict or need for explanations, we can savor our smoked bluefish pâté, harpooned swordfish, and truffle aïoli, too. One could make the observation that today's Nantucketers simply prefer combing the world educating their palates about wine and olive oil to searching for whales and sperm oil.

Secondly, almost every restaurateur profiled here by Samara and Melissa will tell you that he or she came to Nantucket and quickly fell in love with the beauty and quirky ways of the island. When you are overwhelmingly in love, you feel a huge urge to give back to the object of your affections. The talented people interviewed on the pages that follow have all chosen to honor Nantucket's great gift of generosity to them by sharing heartfelt, often sophisticated food and warm hospitality with all fellow lovers of and visitors to this historic faraway island. Behind the scenes, either Melville is magically at work or we're reaping the benefits of a favorite old French proverb: "Without bread, without wine, love is nothing."

—Sarah Leah Chase

The

NANTUCKET
RESTAURANTS

Cookbook

AMERICAN
SEASONS

80 CENTRE STREET

508-228-7111

WWW.AMERICANSEASONS.COM

SEASON: MID-APRIL THROUGH DECEMBER

The name should tip you off.

Even before entering American Seasons, you've probably surmised that chef and co-owner Michael Getter is up to something that reaches beyond the shores of Nantucket. But it's only upon perusing the menu that you realize just how far he's gone. There, you'll find yourself about to embark on a whirlwind tour of four distinct American culinary regions. Discover New England, the Pacific Northwest, the South, and the Southwest, region by region and dish by dish. The menu's extensive offering of appetizers and entrées are to be mixed and matched to create your own custom-tailored, cross-country meal.

For example, you might start out with a braised rabbit torta with jicama relish, red mole, and cilantro crema from the "Wild West" section, or Louisiana crawfish risotto in a fire-roasted onion with fried parsnips in a sweet corn purée from "Down South."

Then, perhaps, continue with a main course of "Pacific Coast" Asian barbecued salmon with sesame potatoes, avocado sauce, and grilled baby bok choy, or seared yellowfin tuna with marinated peppers, linguiça sausage, and native potatoes, under the heading "New England." Tastes from around the world come together at American Seasons, in a melting pot of cuisines that ultimately reaches far and beyond the borders of the United States.

Since 1996, Michael has enjoyed the free range and flexibility offered at American Seasons. He is continually inspired by the menu's unusual format, imagining it as a puzzle in which the challenge is to fit the dishes into the appropriate categories. And, since the dinner menu changes monthly, bringing the four corners of America to Nantucket is an ongoing project. Michael spends a lot of his time gathering ingredients and techniques from around the country and studying the ethnic influences specific to each of the menu's four regions. He's discovered the Portuguese slant to New England cuisine, Asian contributions on the Pacific coast, and the French influence on Southern cooking. If you were to peek into the kitchen's pantry, you would find ingredients ranging from Oregon white truffle oil to hominy grits to chipotle peppers to local New England produce, all of which Michael masterfully employs. His meals, made of only the freshest, highest-quality ingredients, are creatively combined, carefully balanced, and stunningly presented.

But even before Michael took over the kitchen, American Seasons had been a favorite destination of both vacationers and island residents. Tucked discreetly among private homes and historic inns at 80 Centre Street on the outskirts of downtown, the restaurant first opened its imaginative doors in 1988 under the proprietorship of Linda and Everett Reid. They were the ones who developed the signature and then novel regional menu format, quickly establishing quite a following and reputation as one of Nantucket's more unique and outstanding venues. To experience American Seasons for yourself, just follow the plump pink pig, the restaurant's

sign, which points the way to the side entrance of this century-old building, which once served as the neighborhood general store.

Once inside, it's hard not to be struck by its comfortably cozy decor, complete with WPA-style folk-art murals depicting harvest scenes from American farms and a beautiful wooden ceiling, which is actually a resurrected floor from an old Vermont barn. The artfully spattered floors and the tabletops hand-painted with game boards and set with glowing hurricane candle lamps give the bustling restaurant a contemporary yet traditional, decidedly American feel. And the covered outdoor patio, with its cheery copper-topped tables, is perfect for a warm summer evening.

Michael gained his appreciation for fine food at an early age; it was a focal point of his Jewish upbringing in New Jersey. His mother was one of those accomplished home cooks who, as soon as the dishes from one meal were dried and put away, would start dreaming up what to serve at the next one. Growing up, he spent much of his time in the kitchen, helping out Mom or experimenting on his own. The family also took frequent trips to New York to explore its many ethnic restaurants, ex-

Michael Getter and sous-chef Michael LaScola.

posing Michael to myriad cuisines. After-school jobs in kitchens during high school led Michael to a position as sous-chef at the young age of eighteen at Gitane, a small, high-end French restaurant in South Orange, New Jersey, where he helped write the menu from scratch every day. It was an important first experience. He continued his training with two years at the Culinary Institute of America, in Hyde Park, New York, and an externship at La Costa Hotel and Spa in California. Michael then moved to Colorado, where he lived his own version of the American dream, skiing by day and cooking by night. He first arrived on Nantucket in the summer of 1991 with other colleagues who were following the tourist season in a lifestyle that allowed for snowy winters on the slopes and laid-back summers on the water. Nantucket was an obvious choice, with its surfable waters (another of Michael's passions) and abundance of excellent restaurants.

Michael's solid culinary background landed him the position as lead cook with one of Nantucket's very best, 21 Federal, where he worked with chef Kep Sweeney in a challenging and inspiring environment and was soon learning to prepare some of the island's best food. He quickly rose through the ranks to executive chef.

In 1995, Michael caught word that American Seasons was for sale. He seized the opportunity to build on the strong foundation already established by the Reids. In the summer of 1996, Michael and partner Bruce Miller reopened American Seasons. Despite being big news in Nantucket's restaurant community, the change of ownership was relatively seamless in the eyes of American Seasons' clientele. The familiar faces of many returning staff, including sous-chef (and, to this day, right-hand man) Michael LaScola, contributed to the continued loyalty of the patrons who had frequented the restaurant over the years, and the Reids' respected menu format remained outstandingly intact. Michael made his mark modestly, slowly updating American Seasons, lightening up the food and easing the restaurant's image from somewhat rustic to a more sophisticated style.

Michael and his wife, Anne, are now year-round residents of Nantucket. He keeps the restaurant open from April through December and during the winter takes a much-needed break, spending his time reading, traveling, researching, and renovating. During the busy season, for the few hours a day that Michael is not at the restaurant, you're likely to find him out at Cisco Beach with the rest of the surfers, looking to catch that perfect wave.

MENU

Soft Ravioli of Mascarpone and
Walnuts in Mushroom Broth with
Chanterelles and White Truffle Oil

Herb-Roasted Vegetable Tian with
Mâche, Aged Balsamic, Basil Pesto, and
"Sweet 100" Cherry Tomatoes

Local Day-Boat Cod with Fingerling
Potatoes and Leeks in Lobster Broth
with Fennel and Red Onion Salad
and Jersey Peas

Caramelized Nectarine Tart

Soft Ravioli of Mascarpone and Walnuts in Mushroom Broth with Chanterelles and White Truffle Oil

This rich, earthy first course is relatively easy to prepare since the mushroom broth, roasted chanterelles, and ravioli can all be made a day in advance. Then it's simply a matter of putting all the components together.

Serves 6

FOR THE RAVIOLI

- ¾ cup chopped toasted walnuts
- 1½ cups mascarpone cheese
- 2 egg yolks
- ½ teaspoon chopped fresh rosemary, thyme, or oregano
- ½ teaspoon kosher salt
- 36 wonton wrappers (see Note, page 10)
- 1 egg yolk, lightly beaten
  Cornstarch, to sprinkle
- 3 tablespoons white truffle oil
  Minced fresh chives, for garnish

FOR THE MUSHROOM BROTH

- 1½ tablespoons olive oil
- 3 ounces shiitake mushrooms, cleaned and sliced, stems included
- 3 ounces portobello mushrooms, cleaned and sliced, stems included
- 1½ cups chopped white onions
- 1½ cups chopped celery
- 1½ cups chopped carrots
- 1 tablespoon chopped garlic
- 1½ tablespoons chopped mixed fresh herbs such as rosemary, thyme, and oregano
- 2 quarts chicken stock or water
- 1 tablespoon sugar
- ½ tablespoon kosher salt

3 ounces fresh chanterelles, cleaned and trimmed

½ tablespoon olive oil

Salt and freshly ground black pepper, to taste

1. To prepare the ravioli filling, in a large bowl, gently stir together the toasted walnuts, mascarpone, 2 egg yolks, herbs, and salt. Chill for at least 6 hours, preferably overnight. The filling must be very cold in order for the ravioli to hold their shape when cooked.

2. To prepare the mushroom broth, in a stockpot, over medium-high heat, warm the olive oil. Add the mushrooms, onions, celery, carrots, garlic, and herbs and sauté until the vegetables are tender, about 7 minutes. Add the stock, reduce the heat to low, and simmer for 1½ hours. Cool at room temperature.

3. Strain the broth through a fine sieve, discarding the solids, and stir in the sugar and salt. Set aside.

4. Preheat the oven to 400°F. To prepare the chanterelles, spread them out on a baking sheet and sprinkle with olive oil, salt, and pepper. Roast for 5 minutes, then transfer the baking sheet to a wire rack and set aside.

5. Line several baking sheets with parchment paper. On a dry work surface, lay out 3 wonton wrappers. Using a pastry brush or your finger, brush the beaten egg yolk around the outside edge of each wonton wrapper, then spoon 1 tablespoon of the filling into the center of each wrapper. Lay a wonton wrapper on top of each and press firmly but gently around the filling, making sure there are no air pockets. Using a 3-inch cookie cutter, cut the ravioli into circles, then transfer them to a baking sheet and sprinkle with cornstarch. Repeat this process with the remaining wonton wrappers and filling. Refrigerate until ready to cook, up to 24 hours.

6. In a large pot over medium-high heat, bring the broth to a simmer. Add the ravioli in small batches and simmer gently for about 3 minutes per batch.

7. Using a slotted spoon, remove the ravioli and divide them among six soup plates. When all

Wild Mushrooms

Wild mushrooms are overwhelmingly more flavorful than their counterparts, the common supermarket "button" mushroom. If you can't find chanterelles, you may substitute other wild mushrooms, such as porcini, shiitakes, oysters, or morels. Or, try an exotic cultivated mushroom, such as cremini (also known as immature portobellos), which are bred to have an excellent "wild" taste.

the ravioli have been cooked, pour ⅓ cup of the mushroom broth over each portion. Sprinkle the chanterelles over the ravioli, drizzle each plate with ½ tablespoon truffle oil, and garnish with a sprinkling of chives.

Note: *Paper-thin wonton wrappers are often sold in 1-pound packages that contain about 90 wrappers. It's okay to buy more than you need, since the rest can be frozen for at least a month.*

Herb-Roasted Vegetable Tian with Mâche, Aged Balsamic, Basil Pesto, and "Sweet 100" Cherry Tomatoes

This dish evolved as a collaboration with sous-chef Michael LaScola. In the summertime Getter and LaScola like to keep the food light and simple to showcase the perfectly fresh produce they are able to get. Although the word tian *usually describes a homey vegetable casserole, here the vegetables are roasted, then trimmed into neat rounds and stacked into a tower. For a more casual presentation, simply mound the vegetables in the center of the plate. They will taste just as delicious.*

Serves 6 to 8

FOR THE TIAN

4 small eggplants (no larger than 5 inches in diameter), sliced into ½-inch rounds

Olive oil, for drizzling

Kosher salt and freshly ground black pepper, to taste

3 medium red onions, sliced into ¼-inch rounds

6 large red bell peppers

8 medium portobello mushroom caps

¼ cup chopped mixed fresh herbs such as rosemary, thyme, and oregano

FOR THE BASIL PESTO

1 small garlic clove

¾ cup toasted walnuts or pine nuts

½ cup olive oil, plus additional for drizzling

2 cups tightly packed basil leaves

1 teaspoon salt, or to taste

Freshly ground black pepper, to taste

FOR SERVING

2 cups cleaned mâche or watercress

Aged balsamic vinegar, for drizzling

1 pint "Sweet 100" cherry tomatoes, or regular cherry tomatoes, halved

1. Preheat the oven to 475°F. To prepare the tian, arrange the eggplant rounds in one layer on a baking sheet. Sprinkle with a little olive oil, salt, and pepper. Place the onion slices on another sheet and sprinkle with olive oil, salt, and pepper. Roast the vegetables in the oven for 15 to 20 minutes, or until tender.

2. Cut the tops and bottoms off the peppers. Make a vertical slice down one side of each and open them up into  long rectangles. Remove the seeds and membranes. Arrange the peppers on a baking sheet, skin side up. Arrange the mushroom caps, stem side down, on another baking sheet. Sprinkle the vegetables with a little olive oil, salt, pepper, and the chopped herbs. Roast in the oven for 15 to 20 minutes, or until tender. When done, skin the peppers and, using a small knife, trim them into rounds the size of the portobello mushrooms.

3. To prepare the basil pesto, in a food processor, combine the garlic, nuts, and ¼ cup of the oil, and blend to a smooth paste. Add another ¼ cup of the oil, mix well, then add the basil and blend until smooth. Add salt and pepper. The pesto may be made up to a day ahead and stored in the refrigerator, tightly covered.

4. If you want perfectly shaped tians, cut the roasted vegetables into rounds with a 3-inch cookie cutter. Place a round of eggplant in the center of a plate. Top it with a slice of pepper and, with the back of a spoon, spread with a thin layer of pesto. Add a mushroom cap, an onion slice, another eggplant, more pesto, and top with another pepper. Top the stack with a pile of fresh mâche or watercress, drizzle with olive oil and balsamic vinegar, and arrange the tomatoes around the salad.

Local Day-Boat Cod with Fingerling Potatoes and Leeks in Lobster Broth with Fennel and Red Onion Salad and Jersey Peas

New England cod is Michael's favorite fish, especially when it's delivered fresh off the Nantucket day boat. The light lobster broth is heady and delicious, adding lobster's essence without masking the bright flavors of the other ingredients.

Serves 8

FOR THE VEGETABLES

Salt

12 medium fingerling or red bliss potatoes, quartered lengthwise

2 cups fresh or frozen peas

4 fennel bulbs, trimmed

2 large red onions, peeled

FOR THE VINAIGRETTE

⅓ cup red wine vinegar

1 teaspoon sugar

1 teaspoon kosher salt

Freshly ground black pepper, to taste

1 teaspoon chopped mixed fresh herbs such as rosemary, thyme, and oregano

1 cup olive oil

FOR THE LOBSTER BROTH

4 pounds lobster shells

2 tablespoons vegetable oil

8 to 10 celery stalks, roughly chopped

6 carrots, peeled and roughly chopped

3 medium white onions, roughly chopped

½ cup chopped mixed fresh herbs such as rosemary, thyme, and oregano

4 garlic cloves, chopped

1 gallon chicken stock or water

½ cup brandy

6 tablespoons paprika

3 tablespoons sugar

2 tablespoons salt, or to taste

CONTINUED

Eight 7-ounce fresh cod fillets (1 inch
thick)

Salt and freshly ground black pepper,
to taste

3   tablespoons olive oil
Flour, for dusting

8   tablespoons (1 stick) unsalted butter,
cut into bits

4   leeks, white section only, cleaned and
cut into ½-inch-thick half-moons

2   tablespoons chopped mixed fresh
herbs such as rosemary, thyme, and
oregano

1. To prepare the vegetables, fill a large pot with salted water and bring to a boil. Add the
    potatoes and cook for 8 minutes, or until slightly soft. Using a slotted spoon, transfer
    the potatoes to a baking tray to cool and bring the salted water back to a boil.

2. Fill a large bowl with cold water and ice cubes. Add the peas to the boiling water and
    blanch for 1 minute, then transfer them to the ice bath. Drain the peas, transfer them
    to a bowl, and set aside.

3. With a sharp knife, remove the inner core of each fennel bulb. Using a mandoline (or
    a food processor fitted with the thinnest slicing blade), slice the fennel very thin and
    store in cold water to prevent browning. Slice the onions very thin starting on the side
    opposite the root end. Set aside.

4. For the vinaigrette, whisk together the vinegar, sugar, salt, pepper, and herbs until the
    sugar and salt are dissolved. Slowly drizzle in the oil, whisking until incorporated, and
    set aside.

5. Preheat the oven to 400°F. To prepare the lobster broth, wash the lobster shells thor-
    oughly. Place them on a baking tray and roast for 20 minutes. Break up the shells and
    set aside. Keep the oven at 400°F.

6. In a large pot over medium-high heat, warm the oil. Add the celery, carrots, onions,
    herbs, and garlic and sauté for 3 minutes. Add the chicken stock, brandy, lobster shells,
    and paprika. Reduce the heat to low and simmer for 2 hours. Strain the broth through
    a fine sieve, discarding the solids. Add the sugar and salt to the broth, then set the
    broth aside and keep it warm. (This may be made a day ahead and reheated.)

7. To prepare the cod, season the cod fillets with salt and pepper. In a large sauté pan over
    high heat, add enough olive oil to coat the bottom. When a light smoke forms, lightly
    flour the presentation side of each fillet, shaking off any excess. Place as many fillets as
    will fit comfortably, floured side down, in the hot oil and give a slight shake to keep the
    fish from sticking to the bottom. Sauté for 3 minutes, or until nicely browned. Flip the

fish over and place browned side up on a baking tray. Place in the oven for about 5 minutes, or until the fillets are lightly flaky.

8. In a medium sauté pan, over medium heat, melt the butter. Add the leeks and sauté for 1 minute. Add the chopped herbs, cooked potatoes, and salt. Heat until warm, about 2 minutes. Place a pile of the leeks and potatoes in the center of each soup plate, place a fish fillet on top, and ladle some of the lobster broth around the vegetables. Sprinkle some of the peas into the broth. In a bowl, toss the fennel and onions with the vinaigrette, and place a portion of the salad on top of the fish. Serve immediately.

Caramelized Nectarine Tart

This is a great ending to a summertime meal. If you have perfectly ripe nectarines you needn't poach them. just slip off their skins. At the restaurant. the tart is caramelized with a blowtorch. but a broiler works just as well.

Serves 8

FOR THE DOUGH

2¼ cups all-purpose flour

¾ teaspoon salt

½ teaspoon granulated sugar

8 tablespoons (1 stick) plus 3 teaspoons unsalted butter. slightly softened and cut into pieces

1 large egg

1 teaspoon milk

FOR THE PASTRY CREAM

6 large egg yolks

½ cup plus 1 teaspoon granulated sugar

2 tablespoons all-purpose flour

1 cup milk

1 vanilla bean. split lengthwise

1 tablespoon confectioners' sugar

FOR THE NECTARINES

1½ quarts simple syrup (see Note, page 17)

1½ pounds fresh nectarines, halved and pitted

¼ cup granulated sugar

Whipped cream. for serving

1. To make the dough, in a food processor fitted with the metal blade, add the flour, salt, and sugar and pulse to mix. Add the butter pieces and pulse until the mixture resembles coarse crumbs. In a small bowl, combine the egg and milk and beat lightly. Add the egg mixture to the food processor and pulse until just combined. Form the dough into a disk, wrap in plastic, and refrigerate until well chilled, at least 3 hours, or overnight.

2. On a well-floured surface, roll out the dough to a circle about ¼ inch thick and fit it into a 10-inch tart pan. Trim any excess dough and chill the crust for 20 minutes.

3. Meanwhile, prepare the pastry cream. In the bowl of an electric mixer fitted with the whisk attachment, beat the yolks and one third of the sugar until the sugar is dissolved and the mixture is pale and forms a slight ribbon when the beaters are lifted, about 3 minutes. Sift in the flour and mix well.

4. In a saucepan over high heat, combine the remaining sugar, the milk, and the split vanilla bean and bring to a simmer. Remove the pan from the heat and slowly pour one third of the milk mixture into the egg mixture, whisking constantly. Pour the egg-milk mixture back into the milk, stirring constantly. Return the pan to the stove over medium-low heat and cook the custard, stirring constantly, until it thickens enough to coat the back of a spoon. Strain the custard into a bowl, sprinkle with the confectioners' sugar, and chill for about 4 hours, until cold.

5. To prepare the nectarines, in a large saucepan over high heat bring the simple syrup to a simmer. Add the fruit, being careful not to splash, and poach the nectarines for about 5 minutes, until tender but still firm. Remove with a slotted spoon and peel the fruit when cool enough to handle.

6. Preheat the oven to 400°F. Spread the chilled pastry cream evenly over the bottom of the crust. Arrange the nectarine halves evenly on top and sprinkle with the sugar. Bake for 20 to 25 minutes, until the crust is golden around the edges. Transfer the tart to a wire rack to cool.

7. Just before serving, preheat the broiler. Broil the tart until the cream turns golden brown, about 1 to 2 minutes. Watch carefully so the tart doesn't burn. Alternately, use a blowtorch to brown the tart. Serve the tart with whipped cream.

Note: *To make 6 cups of simple syrup. in a heavy saucepan combine 4 cups of sugar with 4 cups of water and stir over high heat until the sugar has dissolved. Let the syrup come to a boil. then simmer for 1 more minute and remove from the heat. Allow the syrup to cool before using. Simple syrup can be kept indefinitely in a tightly covered container in the refrigerator.*

BLACK-EYED
SUSAN'S

10 INDIA STREET

508-325-0308

SEASON: APRIL THROUGH OCTOBER

This little thirty-two-seat restaurant doesn't advertise, take reservations, or have a published phone number, yet there's a crowd that spills onto the narrow brick sidewalks of India Street almost every night and morning of the week from April through October. What's all the affectionate buzz about? It must be the restaurant's friendly, neighborhood feel, coupled with its outstanding food, that has kept grateful locals and curious tourists alike flocking to Black-Eyed's since its first season in 1993. Proprietress extraordinaire Susan Handy and her partner, chef Jeff Worster, have carved a perfect niche for their brilliant, creative, ethnically influenced food, in a venue that gracefully bridges the gap between Nantucket's family-style eateries and its many excellent upscale restaurants. At Black-Eyed's, food is presented in a casual rustic setting at affordable prices. It is just the sort of funky space you might expect to find in a hip New York City or Los Angeles neighborhood. But, lucky for Nantucket, it's smack in the heart of downtown.

Inside, it's a lively scene. Susan, always wearing something enviable, greets friends and regulars, wielding her ever-growing waiting list at the door and on the street. Meanwhile, Jeff and his crew put on a show in their open kitchen, sautéing up a storm. Thankfully, the ten small but comfortable tables are close enough for a glimpse of the high-flying action. Pine-paneled walls keep the space warm and inviting, and eclectic green and purple chandeliers, rescued from the tea-party heyday of the White Elephant resort, add just the right touch of eccentricity and Nantucket history to the room.

Twenty-five years before 10 India Street became Black-Eyed Susan's, it saw its share of coffee cups and chowder bowls pass over the counter, first as the Dory and then as Two Steps Up. It was during those early years that Susan, a third-generation California girl from Los Angeles, was busy traveling the world, exploring and eating her way through Europe, Southeast Asia, and the South Pacific. In 1983, when a fellow traveler invited her to the island for a summer of sailing, she jumped at the chance. "It was just magical," says Susan, recalling her first glimpse of Nantucket from the ferry on a sparkling July day. She lived on a farm in Polpis, sailed by day, and hung out at the Straight Wharf Bar by night. She was quickly hooked, but she needed to make a living.

No stranger to gourmet cooking, Susan inherited her love of fine food and entertaining from her mother, who devoured *Bon Appétit* magazines and signed up for every cooking class she could find—in fact, more

than she had the time to attend. Susan often found herself going in her busy mother's place. She got the chance to put her food knowledge to the test years later, working on an archaeological dig in New Mexico, where she spent three years as the camp manager responsible for feeding twenty-five co-workers out in the field, with no refrigeration.

Compared to that challenge, feeding the locals on Nantucket sounded easy. So, in 1984 Susan leapt when she was offered charge of an authentic soda-counter concession at Congdon's Pharmacy on Main Street, one of the island's two competing next-door pharmacy lunch counters. The California girl immediately improved upon the fare, adding fresh and homegrown ingredients to the mix. Everyone in town sits down at these lunch counters from time to time, and three years and a lot of good gossip and great sandwiches later, Susan was ensconced in the community.

It was at the Boarding House, another local institution, that Susan first met and worked with Jeff Worster. Jeff had landed on Nantucket by way of traditional Maine fish houses and inns, and after stints in Boston at the Backyard and the Brookline Country Club. During the summer of 1986 at the Boarding House, Jeff worked closely with then executive chef Sarah Leah Chase, who was dazzling diners with her innovative "new American" cuisine. Sarah's inspiring creations, with their risk-taking combinations of ingredients, eclectic ethnic flavors, and, most of all, lack of traditional boundaries, solidified Jeff's passion for cooking. It was the summer of 1987 when Susan, then working as a waitress at the Boarding House and dreaming of having a place of her own, took notice. Susan liked

Susan Handy and Jeff Worster.

BLACK-EYED
SUSAN'S

Jeff's style and hinted that when she found the perfect place, she'd like him to be her chef.

In the early spring of 1993, Two Steps Up was suddenly available for lease. Susan, seeing a diamond in the rough, grabbed at the opportunity. She and Jeff took the plunge, scrubbing the space from top to bottom, painting and updating the kitchen equipment, and giving it all a more contemporary look. They opened Black-Eyed Susan's a mere three weeks later. At first they just served the most unusual breakfasts on island. Forget eggs over easy. Eggs were scrambled with tons of fresh cilantro, and black-eyed peas, spicy chicken sausage, and tofu scrambles were standard on their menu. Once the pair got a better sense of the rhythm of the place and its quirky, behind-the-counter open kitchen and diner-style griddle, they decided to tackle dinner.

From the get-go, the dinner menu at Black-Eyed Susan's read like a culinary travel journal, taking equally well-traveled customers from Thailand to Mexico, Italy, Africa, and home to New England all in one night and two or three courses. In Jeff's hands, classic ethnic dishes are pared right

down to the basics, then paired up with local ingredients in unexpected combinations.

At Black-Eyed's you can order roast pork Korean-style, on a jasmine rice cake with bok choy–carrot sambal one night, and then find roast pork Mexican-style, with black beans and a refreshing tropical fruit and cabbage slaw another night. Most importantly, all of Jeff's dishes maintain a simplicity that lets you taste every individual element, like his pad thai, with its rich peanut sauce, bright burst of lemon, and deliciously crunchy fresh sprouts.

Portions are always generous and shareable and prices are kept reasonable. It's by choice and not necessity that Susan invites you to BYOB, keeping the meal, when enjoyed with your own wine, more affordable still. The menu changes frequently both to accommodate a captive audience of regulars and to satisfy Jeff's and Susan's culinary wanderlust and fascination with seasonal food. Every year they update Black-Eyed Susan's a touch more, refine the focus of the food a little further, and continue to please an ever-expanding number of devotees.

MENU

Signature Salad with
Morning Glory Chai Vinaigrette
and Sesame Crisps

Tuna Tartare with Cucumbers
and Sriracha Aïoli

Pandemonious Pork with
Citrus Barbecue Sauce, Indonesian Slaw,
and Smoky Black Beans

Lemon Tart with
Spring Strawberry Sorbet

Signature Salad with Morning Glory Chai Vinaigrette and Sesame Crisps

You can purchase chai tea mix at tea shops and health food stores. It includes black tea and a special spice blend. In this recipe chai tea becomes the liquid base for the vinaigrette, which will keep in the refrigerator for up to two weeks.

Serves 4 to 6

FOR THE SALAD

½ cup brewed chai tea

¼ cup seasoned rice wine vinegar

1 tablespoon honey

½ teaspoon Dijon mustard

1½ cups grapeseed oil or light salad oil

½ tablespoon sesame oil

Dash of soy sauce

Salt and freshly ground black pepper,
to taste

1 pound (6 cups) mesclun field greens

½ cup mixed fresh chervil, dill, and
cilantro leaves

Chopped scallions, for garnish

Coarsely ground black pepper, for
garnish

FOR THE SESAME CRISPS

Black and white sesame seeds

1 egg

Dash of water

Dash of sesame oil

8 wonton wrappers

1. In a food processor, blend together the tea, vinegar, honey, and mustard. With the processor running, slowly add the oils to emulsify. Season with soy sauce and salt and pepper. Set the dressing aside.

2. To make the sesame crisps, preheat the oven to 350°F. Sprinkle a nonstick or parchment-lined baking sheet with black and white sesame seeds.

3. Beat the egg with a little water and sesame oil to make an egg wash.

4. Cut the wonton wrappers in half to make triangles. Brush the egg wash on both sides of the wonton triangles. Place on the sesame-sprinkled sheet, and sprinkle the tops with more sesame seeds. Bake for 5 to 7 minutes, turning the pan halfway through cooking. The crisps are done when golden brown.

5. Gently toss the mesclun greens and herbs in the dressing to taste. Mound the greens high on each plate and garnish with sesame crisps and chopped scallions. Sprinkle coarsely ground pepper around the rim of each plate.

Tuna Tartare with Cucumbers and Sriracha Aïoli

This appetizer can also be served as an hors d'oeuvre piled on sesame crackers with a dab of the aïoli on top.

Serves 4

FOR THE CUCUMBERS

1 large cucumber, peeled, sliced lengthwise, seeded, and very thinly sliced into half-moons
Kosher salt

1 teaspoon rice wine vinegar
1 teaspoon vegetable oil
Coarsely ground black pepper, to taste

FOR THE TUNA TARTARE

1 pound fresh sashimi-grade tuna (ahi or yellowfin), cut into ¼-inch cubes
1 shallot, minced
3 tablespoons chili oil, plus more for garnish

2 tablespoons whole capers
1 tablespoon chopped fresh cilantro
Juice of ½ lemon
2 scallions, thinly sliced
Dash of sriracha (see Note, page 27)

FOR THE SRIRACHA AÏOLI

1 tablespoon sriracha
1 tablespoon mayonnaise

Fresh lemon juice, to taste
Pinch of salt

FOR THE GARNISH

1 scallion, chopped
4 sprigs of fresh cilantro

Croutons, optional
Bread rounds or pita triangles

1. Sprinkle the cucumber slices with salt and set them aside for 30 minutes. Drain and toss with the vinegar, oil, and coarsely ground pepper. Set aside to marinate.
2. Within 5 to 10 minutes of serving, make the tuna tartare. In a bowl, combine the tuna, shallot, oil, capers, cilantro, lemon juice, scallions, and sriracha and mix well. Set aside.

3. For the aïoli, in a small bowl, blend together the sriracha, mayonnaise, lemon juice, and salt. Transfer the mixture to a plastic bag with a corner snipped off to pipe the dots.

4. Place a 3-inch cookie cutter in the center of one plate. Drain the marinated cucumbers and fill the bottom of the cutter with one quarter of the cucumbers. Pack one quarter of the seasoned tuna on top. Remove the cutter to unmold. Pipe dots of aïoli and additional chili oil around the plate. Repeat with the remaining ingredients on the other three plates. Garnish the plates with chopped scallion, a sprig of cilantro, and croutons, if desired. Serve with bread rounds or pita triangles.

Note: Sriracha is a Vietnamese chili-garlic sauce. If you can't find it, substitute Szechwan chili paste, which is available at Chinese specialty stores.

Pandemonious Pork with Citrus Barbecue Sauce, Indonesian Slaw, and Smoky Black Beans

With elements of both Asia and Mexico juxtaposed on the plate, this quirky, robust entrée is as delicious as it is unique. At the restaurant it's served with large chunks of fresh warm crusty bread.

Serves 6

FOR THE PORK

6 tablespoons olive oil

One 2-pound pork butt or pork round, trimmed of fat and cut into 4-inch blocks

Salt and freshly ground black pepper, to taste

FOR THE BEANS

1 pound dried black beans

6 cups water

½ pound cubed thick-cut bacon

3 garlic cloves, roughly chopped

2 shallots, thinly sliced

1 teaspoon ground cumin

1 teaspoon chili powder

1 tablespoon butter

Squeeze of fresh lemon juice

Salt and freshly ground black pepper, to taste

FOR THE SLAW

1 small head of white cabbage or ½ head each red and white, finely julienned (about 6 cups)

2 cups small-diced fresh pineapple (from ½ large pineapple)

1 ripe banana, mashed

2 shallots or 1 small red onion, thinly sliced

1 roasted red pepper, thinly sliced

3 tablespoons rice wine vinegar

3 tablespoons fresh lemon juice

1 tablespoon canola or grapeseed oil

1 teaspoon Thai fish sauce

2 sprigs of fresh cilantro, chopped, plus whole sprigs for garnish

Salt and freshly ground black pepper, to taste

1 cup crushed tomatoes or tomato
    purée
½ small mango, peeled and coarsely
    chopped
½ cup fresh orange juice
2 tablespoons fresh lemon juice
2 tablespoons sriracha, or to taste
    (see Note, page 27)

1 garlic clove, roughly chopped
1 teaspoon freshly grated gingerroot
½ cup light brown sugar
¼ cup red wine vinegar
1 tablespoon soy sauce or tamari
1 teaspoon ground cumin
    Salt and freshly ground black pepper,
    to taste

1. Preheat the oven to 300°F. In a deep, heavy pan with a lid, warm 3 tablespoons of the oil over high heat. Salt and pepper the pork, add to the pan, and cook until brown on all sides. Add enough water to cover the pork by 1 inch. Cover the pan and place it in the oven for about 2½ hours, or until the pork is tender and pulls apart easily. Once cooled, the pork can be stored in the refrigerator for up to 2 days in its own liquid.

2. In a large pot, combine the beans and water and simmer, uncovered, for 1 hour or until just tender, adding more water whenever necessary.

3. Meanwhile, in a large bowl, combine all of the ingredients for the slaw and toss well. Let the mixture sit so the flavors can develop, at least 1 hour. Adjust the seasonings to taste.

4. To finish the beans, in a skillet over medium heat, sauté the bacon until crisp, about 8 minutes. Add the garlic and shallots and sauté for 1 minute longer. Add the cooked beans, cumin, and chili powder to the pan and bring the mixture to a simmer. Add the butter, lemon juice, and salt and pepper. Keep warm.

5. To make the barbecue sauce, in a large saucepan over high heat, combine the tomatoes, mango, orange juice, lemon juice, sriracha, garlic, and ginger and bring to a boil. Reduce the heat to medium, partially cover the pan, and simmer for 15 minutes. Add the sugar, vinegar, soy sauce, cumin, and salt and pepper. Simmer for another 2 to 3 minutes, or until the sauce thickens. Strain the sauce into a bowl and reserve.

6. After the pork has been cooked and cooled, shred it into 1-inch chunks. In a large skillet, heat the remaining 3 tablespoons of oil until smoking hot. Add the pork and sauté it until it is brown and crisp on all sides. Season with salt and pepper.

7. To serve, mound the beans in the bottom of each bowl and spoon in chunks of pork. Drizzle with barbecue sauce, top with a mound of slaw, and garnish with sprigs of cilantro.

Lemon Tart with
Spring Strawberry Sorbet

A wedge of lemon tart topped with a scoop of icy sorbet makes a sweet yet refreshing ending to a delicious dinner. This recipe calls for an ice-cream maker to process the sorbet. If you don't have one, be sure to buy the best available store brand of sorbet.

Serves 8

FOR THE CRUST

1½ cups all-purpose flour

½ tablespoon sugar

⅛ teaspoon salt

12 tablespoons (1½ sticks) unsalted butter,
    chilled and cubed

1½ tablespoons heavy cream

1 egg yolk, lightly beaten

FOR THE FILLING

10 egg yolks

1 cup fresh lemon juice (from about
    4 to 5 lemons), strained

¾ cup sugar

½ cup water

Pinch of salt

4 tablespoons (½ stick) unsalted
    butter, chilled and cubed

FOR THE SORBET

1 quart fresh strawberries, sliced

1½ cups simple syrup (see Note, page 17)

1. To make the crust, in a food processor fitted with the metal blade, pulse the flour, sugar, and salt with the butter until the mixture resembles coarse crumbs. Add the cream and egg yolk and pulse until just combined. Transfer the dough to a floured board and form it into a disk. Wrap in plastic and refrigerate for at least 1 hour or up to 4 days.

2. Preheat the oven to 350°F. Roll out the dough to a 12-inch circle and fit it into a 10-inch tart pan; trim the edges. Cover the dough with foil and fill with beans or pie

weights. Bake for 20 minutes. Remove the foil and weights and bake for 10 to 15 minutes longer, or until the crust is golden brown. Transfer to a wire rack to cool.

3. To make the filling, in the top of a double boiler over simmering water, whisk together the egg yolks, lemon juice, sugar, water, and salt. Cook, whisking constantly and gently, until the mixture becomes thick and custardy. Turn off the heat and whisk in the butter. Pour the filling through a fine sieve into the prebaked tart shell. Let the tart chill in the refrigerator for at least 1 hour and up to 24 hours.

4. To make the sorbet, in a food processor fitted with the metal blade, purée the strawberries. Pass the purée through a fine sieve and stir in the simple syrup. Freeze the mixture in an ice-cream machine according to the manufacturer's directions.

5. To serve the tart, preheat the broiler. Broil the tart until the top turns a speckled brown. Cut the tart into wedges and serve with the sorbet.

BOARDING HOUSE

12 FEDERAL STREET

508-228-9622

SEASON: YEAR-ROUND

THE PEARL

12 FEDERAL STREET

508-228-9701

SEASON: APRIL THROUGH DECEMBER

If you're thinking of stopping by the historic Boarding House for a simple bowl of good old-fashioned island clam chowder, you'd better take a look at the menu. Located on a bustling corner in the heart of downtown Nantucket, the Boarding House serves dinner year-round—but if you're picturing the standard fare of a New England inn as the name suggests, you're in for a palate-awakening surprise. On any given summer evening, the restaurant's low-ceilinged dining room, bustling bar, and patio are festive and jam-packed with locals and tourists alike—but it is tempura-battered asparagus spears and not fried clams with tartar sauce that sate revelers.

Although neither of the restaurant's proprietors, Angela and Seth Raynor, grew up near Nantucket (Seth is from Long Island, Angela from Wisconsin), it's no surprise that they now make the island their home. It was Seth who was first seduced by

Nantucket's charm and drawn by its amazing restaurant scene. After attending the New England Culinary Institute, where he and Angela met as students, he came to Nantucket to work for the renowned Jean-Charles Berruet at the Chanticleer. There, he absorbed classical French techniques and learned the importance of "food coordination." Meanwhile, Angela was working in France, at a restaurant called Le Petit Prince, near Grasse. Hundreds of dollars' worth of phone conversations later, Angela flew from Nice to Nantucket and took a job working in the front of the house at the Chanticleer. Several years later, after the couple had married and both had worked in different venues around the island, the venerable old Boarding House came up for sale. The restaurant had already been through three successful "generations." It was first opened by Ben Ardrey, then taken over by Jimmy Perelman, and passed to Bob Kuratek and Sarah Leah Chase. The couple didn't have to think twice, and in 1992 they opened the doors.

For almost ten years Seth has managed to keep the menu fresh, yet true to the parameters he and Angela outlined when they wrote their first menu. The focus is still on local produce and seafood, and the technique can best be described as new American, informed by French, mainly Provençal, sensibilities and enlivened by Asian flavors. Sure, they sometimes serve a chowder, but it's more likely to be a light melding of Tuckernuck lobster, fresh-shucked corn, and Yukon Gold potatoes, drizzled with an extravagant splash of truffle oil.

This sort of inventive flair is typical of Seth's menu. The veal chop at the Boarding House is clearly influenced by his and Angela's love for Provence. It is served with mashed potatoes and a thyme jus, yet Seth adds flavor to the plate with an Asian element: spiced tempura onion rings. Atlantic salmon arrives at the table via the Pacific Ocean, atop soba noodles, with straw mushrooms and a sesame aïoli.

The unusual combinations on the menu demand an equally eclectic and customized wine list, and Angela has built up just the right cellar for this purpose. The compatibility of the international selection of wines has earned the Boarding House a *Wine Spectator* Award every year since the Raynors took over. Angela's cultivated knowledge of wines and her superb manner as a hostess are a treat, and are even more

praiseworthy when you consider that she is an accomplished chef as well.

Although she prefers the entertaining, front-of-the-house side of the industry, Angela was honored along with Seth as Outstanding Alumni by their alma mater, the New England Culinary Institute. This talented couple enjoys traveling extensively in Europe and Asia, tasting, and brainstorming. The ideas they bring back from their travels are often filtered into their menus. During the winter, natives enjoy sneak previews of new dishes during the "testing" phase, before the dishes debut during the high-volume season.

If you peek into the cramped Boarding House kitchen, you'll understand the true immensity of Seth's accomplishments—providing so many people with consistent and inspiring food, all from a kitchen barely large enough to flip a flapjack in! But there are limits to what the Boarding House's cramped kitchen can handle. That's why, after eight years at the restaurant, Angela and Seth began to look around for a space where they could stretch, both physically and culinarily. When the florist who rented the building's second floor, above the restaurant, let them know that he would be moving to nearby Chestnut Street, they were thrilled. They had been looking to buy rather than rent a new restaurant, and what should present itself but the space they already owned!

The building's top two floors became the Pearl restaurant. With the help of architect Chris Smith, Angela transformed the interior into an elegant underwater fantasy that envelops you as soon as you step through the doors. On the outside, the handsome, painstakingly preserved Federal Revival building gives no hint of the imaginative splendor of the interior. But once inside, you are bathed in the watery glow of immense saltwater aquariums. The dining room is painted in pale blue sea tones, while the opalescent booths and huge, pearl-shaped light fixture recessed into the ceiling make you feel that the world is indeed your oyster.

Seth and Angela Raynor.

Considering the minuscule kitchen of the Boarding House, it's no wonder that the Pearl's kitchen is a dream, built to Seth's specifications. As a special perk, the Pearl offers a chef's garden table (seating six to eight) on the lovely deck behind the kitchen. It affords a front-row view of the action on the line through glass French doors. For a more secluded, intimate dining experience, there's also the upstairs private dining room, which seats ten to sixteen, while more social diners might opt for the conviviality of the stylish alabaster-onyx bar.

Among the superb creations regularly featured on the menu are a monumental fresh seafood plateau, a delicate warm oyster salad in truffle-oil vinaigrette, a Thai curried native lobster soup, and an exquisite entrée of seared sushi-grade tuna with jasmine rice, stir-fried vegetables, and wasabi tamari. Pastry chef Jodi Levesque does justice to these delicacies with finales like her Black Pearl, a decadent chocolate torte in crème caramel sauce.

Dave Buchman is now the executive chef at the Boarding House, while Seth concentrates more on the Pearl. Dave is completely in sync with Seth's thinking, and his taking over the reins was more of a continuum than a transition. The amazing part is that Angela, Seth, and Dave can really keep two establishments of such high caliber yet different temperaments operating simultaneously. And it's even more amazing when you meet them. The Raynors are friendly, down-to-earth people and loving parents, who take vacations and spend as much time as possible with their two young children. But, wherever this couple goes, you can be sure that they're cataloging their experiences, either to subtly enrich the Boarding House menu or to make a new splash at the Pearl.

MENU

Osetra Scallops

Cold Tomato Infusion with Lobster

Asparagus with Red Wine Vinaigrette
and Tomato Bruschetta

Pan-Roasted Atlantic Halibut
with Wild Mushroom Broth,
Pea Tendrils, and Truffle Aïoli

Fresh Raspberry Martini with
Tart Citrus Mousse

Osetra Scallops

The creamy, sweet combination of scallops and crème fraîche is luxuriously garnished with salty little "pearls" of caviar.

Serves 4

8 large sea scallops (see sidebar, page 39)

5 tablespoons extra-virgin olive oil

1 tablespoon unsalted butter

2 leeks, whites and tender green parts only, well washed and cut into 2-inch pieces

Salt

1 cup crème fraîche

2 tablespoons vodka

Freshly ground black pepper, to taste

2 ounces osetra caviar

Fresh chives, for garnish

1. Rinse the scallops briefly, then blot them gently with paper towels and set aside.
2. In a heavy saucepan over medium-low heat, heat 2 tablespoons of the oil and the tablespoon of butter until melted; add the leeks and cook until tender, about 5 minutes. Lightly season the leeks with salt, then add 1 to 2 tablespoons of water and cover the pot. Let the leeks continue to cook, covered, until they are completely soft and have lost their green color, about 30 minutes. Set aside and keep warm.
3. In a bowl, combine the crème fraîche and vodka, and set aside.
4. Season the scallops with salt and pepper. In a heavy skillet, heat the remaining 3 tablespoons of oil over medium-high heat. Add the scallops and sauté for about 1 ½ minutes on each side.
5. Place a spoonful of the warm braised leeks on each plate and top with 2 scallops. Put a dollop of the crème fraîche and vodka mixture on top of each scallop. Garnish with a small spoonful of the caviar and snip some fresh chives over each plate.

Scallops

Scallops are a reason to have a good relationship with your fishmonger. To be certain you are choosing good shucked sea scallops, look for cream- or pinkish-hued flesh and an odor that is not overpowering. You are of course looking for the freshest scallop available, but because scallop boats go out for over a week at a time, fast-frozen sea scallops may actually taste fresher than somewhat dehydrated fresh scallops that have been soaked to plump them up again.

Live sea scallops are sometimes available in specialty markets and are worth the price. The shells should close up when you squeeze down on them, and they should smell fresh, not fishy. To shuck a live scallop, slide the blade of a sharp knife along the top shell to detach the scallop without cutting into it. Use the knife to detach the scallop from the bottom shell, then pull away the membrane and viscera that surround the scallop.

Cold Tomato Infusion with Lobster

Crabmeat can be substituted for the lobster in this fragrant tomato soup.

Serves 4

3 large ripe tomatoes, cored and
   quartered

2 tablespoons sherry vinegar

½ teaspoon kosher salt, or to taste

¼ teaspoon freshly ground black pepper,
   plus more to taste

¼ cup extra-virgin olive oil

1½ tablespoons white truffle oil

4 to 8 ounces cooked lobster meat
   (see sidebar, page 77), cubed

¼ cup mayonnaise, crème fraîche, or
   mascarpone

   Strained fresh lemon juice, to taste

1. In a blender, purée the quartered tomatoes with the vinegar, salt, and pepper until they are completely smooth. Slowly add the olive and truffle oils and blend until the mixture is well combined. Strain the mixture through a fine sieve lined with cheesecloth, discarding the solids, and refrigerate for at least 4 hours before serving.

2. In a bowl, combine the seafood and mayonnaise, crème fraîche, or mascarpone. Season with a hint of lemon juice and adjust the salt and pepper. Chill until ready to serve.

3. Spoon the tomato infusion into individual bowls. Place a spoonful of seafood in the center of each and serve.

The Pearl.

Asparagus with Red Wine Vinaigrette and Tomato Bruschetta

Deep-frying asparagus brings out their rich, savory flavor, which is perfectly balanced by a bright vinaigrette. The tomato bruschetta rounds out this appetizer while keeping it light and summery.

Serves 4

FOR THE VINAIGRETTE

3 tablespoons red wine vinegar

2 tablespoons Dijon mustard

½ cup canola oil

¼ cup extra-virgin olive oil

FOR THE BRUSCHETTA

2 tomatoes, seeded and diced

Salt and freshly ground black pepper, to taste

2 tablespoons extra-virgin olive oil

1 tablespoon minced fresh herbs, such as chives, basil, or thyme

Toasted baguette slices

FOR THE ASPARAGUS

3 cups peanut oil, for frying

1½ pounds asparagus, cleaned and trimmed

Salt and freshly ground black pepper, to taste

1. To prepare the vinaigrette, in a blender, whirl the vinegar and mustard. Add the canola oil and olive oil in a slow stream, blending to combine. Set aside.
2. To make the bruschetta, in a medium bowl, combine the tomatoes with salt and pepper. Transfer to a strainer and let sit for 1 hour to drain away excess liquid. Return the tomatoes to the bowl and gently stir in the olive oil and herbs.
3. In a large saucepan over medium-high heat, heat the peanut oil to 350°F. Add the asparagus and fry for 1½ minutes, until they are bright green and slightly blistered. Transfer to paper towels to drain. Season with salt and pepper.

4. To serve, arrange the asparagus in the center of each plate, add a toasted baguette slice to both sides of the asparagus, and mound some tomato salad on each of the bread toasts. Drizzle red wine vinaigrette over the asparagus.

A Boarding House mainstay.

Pan-Roasted Atlantic Halibut with Wild Mushroom Broth, Pea Tendrils, and Truffle Aïoli

You can use any available wild or exotic mushrooms, such as shiitake, oyster mushrooms, portobello, or cremini, to make the broth.

Serves 4

FOR THE MUSHROOM BROTH

- 2 tablespoons extra-virgin olive oil
- 2 shallots, sliced
- 4 cups wild or exotic mushrooms, cleaned and sliced
- 2 tablespoons unsalted butter
- 2 sprigs of fresh thyme
- 1 quart chicken stock
- 1 quart water
- Salt and freshly ground black pepper, to taste

FOR THE AÏOLI

- 1 large egg
- 1 large egg yolk
- 2 garlic cloves, peeled
- 1 tablespoon fresh lemon juice, strained
- 1 tablespoon kosher salt
- 1/8 teaspoon cracked black pepper, or to taste
- 1¼ cups plus 2 tablespoons extra-virgin olive oil
- ¼ cup truffle oil
- 2 tablespoons water, if needed

FOR THE HALIBUT

- 2 tablespoons canola oil
- Four 6-ounce fillets of Atlantic halibut
- ¼ pound pea shoots (tendrils), washed and dried

1. To make the mushroom broth, in a heavy stockpot, heat the olive oil over medium heat. Add the shallots and cook, stirring occasionally, until tender, about 3 minutes. Add the mushrooms and cook, stirring, until tender, about 5 minutes. Add the butter to the pot and raise the heat to medium-high. Continue to cook, stirring, until the

vegetables begin to caramelize and turn brown, then add the thyme. Pour the stock and water into the pot and swirl to wash down the sides of the pot.

2. Lower the heat to medium and simmer until the soup is reduced by half, about 45 minutes. Strain through a sieve, discarding the solids. Return the soup to the stockpot and season with salt and pepper; keep warm.

3. To make the aïoli, in a blender, combine the egg, egg yolk, garlic, lemon juice, salt, and pepper and blend for 1 minute. With the motor running, slowly drizzle in the olive and truffle oils, blending to combine. If necessary, add up to 2 tablespoons of water, little by little, until the aïoli is smooth. Set aside.

4. Preheat the oven to 450°F. In a large, ovenproof sauté pan, heat the canola oil over high heat. Add the fillets, flesh side down, and sear them for 1 minute, until golden brown. Transfer the pan to the oven and cook for 3 minutes. Turn the fillets over and cook for another 2 minutes, or until the flesh is opaque.

5. To serve, place the fillets in individual soup bowls and ladle 1 cup of the wild mushroom broth over the fish. Drizzle with a spoonful of aïoli and garnish with some of the pea tendrils.

Fresh Raspberry Martini
with Tart Citrus Mousse

Any excess mousse can be kept in the refrigerator for up to five days.

Serves 6

1 cup granulated sugar

²/₃ cup strained fresh lemon juice

8 tablespoons (1 stick) unsalted butter, cut into pieces

1 tablespoon lemon zest

3 large eggs

1½ cups heavy cream

⅓ cup confectioners' sugar

¾ cup fresh raspberries

1. In a saucepan over medium-low heat, whisk the sugar, lemon juice, butter, and zest until the sugar dissolves and the butter melts. Raise the heat to medium-high and let the liquid come to a boil, without stirring.

2. In a large bowl, whisk the eggs well, until they are light and frothy.

3. When the lemon mixture has come to a boil, slowly pour the hot liquid into the bowl with the eggs, whisking constantly. Combine well, then return the mixture to the saucepan and cook over low heat, stirring constantly, until the mixture has thickened, about 2 minutes. Do not allow the curd to boil.

4. Transfer the thickened curd to a bowl and let cool. Cover the surface of the curd directly with plastic wrap so a skin does not form. Refrigerate overnight.

5. In the bowl of a mixer fitted with the whisk attachment, whip the heavy cream with the confectioners' sugar until it forms stiff peaks.

6. Gently fold half of the chilled lemon curd into the whipped cream. Reserve the rest for another use. Divide the mousse into martini glasses and serve topped with fresh berries.

THE
CHANTICLEER

9 NEW STREET, 'SCONSET

508-257-6231

WWW.THECHANTICLEERINN.COM

SEASON: MAY THROUGH OCTOBER

Gourmet magazine brought a new appreciation of food to American homes in the 1950s and '60s. It also brought chef Jean-Charles Berruet to Nantucket, and he brought with him fine French dining, the likes of which had not been seen on the island before.

The story begins in France. Jean-Charles spent his childhood in Brittany, cooking family feasts on Sundays alongside his father, who also loved to cook. At the age of fourteen, Jean-Charles decided he wanted to make his passion his profession. With his father's blessing, he began a three-year apprenticeship at the great French restaurant Charles Berrier, in Tours, the center of the Loire, which was named for the chef-owner, who became his teacher. There, he learned both the basics of classic French cuisine and the discipline needed to create it.

Several years and restaurants later,

Jean-Charles, wanting to see more of the world and learn English, moved to England to work at Queen's Hotel in Manchester, where ironically the huge staff was mostly French and the food was traditional Escoffier. But living in England brought Jean-Charles more than a command of the language; it also brought him a wife. Jean-Charles met his wife, Anne, who was from Scotland, at a Wimpy Burger restaurant (of all places), and they married soon after and moved back to France.

Until they landed on Nantucket, their life was constantly in flux, moving across France and working at—and even owning—small family-style restaurants. But it was while working in Verdun, near an American military base, that Jean-Charles's fate was altered.

One of the American officers whom Jean-Charles had grown friendly with gave him his first copy of *Gourmet* magazine.

Since the Berruets were considering a move to the States, Jean-Charles decided to write to the editor, asking if he had any suggestions for a relocating chef. Earle MacAusland, founder of the magazine, wrote back to say that his chef had just left—would Jean-Charles like the job? Jean-Charles interviewed at *Gourmet's* Paris bureau and landed the position, and he and Anne flew to New York City, eager to see the sights and begin their new life. When they arrived with $300, two suitcases, and their young son, Mark, they didn't know a soul. Waiting to meet them was Mr. MacAusland, who drove them to his private plane, and they were flying to Nantucket before they knew what had hit them. The only bit of New York City they saw on that trip was the airport!

Before they arrived, Anne and Jean-Charles had never heard of Nantucket. And as the plane descended upon a bare sand spit, they were terrified! They surveyed the wooden houses, which in France would have only housed peasants, and they wondered what they had gotten themselves into. However, they were most reassured when they were taken to the MacAuslands' home in Shimmo, where Mr. MacAusland and his wife, Jean, spent their summers. The Berruets soon grew to love the beautiful old estate, and they lived and worked there very happily through Jean-Charles's three-year contract.

Working as the MacAuslands' chef, Jean-Charles would write the menu every day, cooking anything he wanted. He had people who flew to Boston or New York to get ingredients for him—anything from fresh produce to foie gras. Anne and Mark stayed full-time on Nantucket, in a house that the MacAuslands rented for them, and they were invited to dinner on Sundays. It was a wonderful life, and Mr. MacAusland and Jean-Charles became great friends.

After his initial shock, Jean-Charles grew to like Nantucket. The island's moors reminded him of his native Brittany, and the family really took root. They made friends easily in the comfortable, small community of the town. After two years, Mr. MacAusland lent them the down payment to buy a house—interest free—and Jean-Charles and Anne had another child, Natalie.

In 1970, when Jean-Charles had fulfilled his contract with the MacAuslands,

Jean-Charles Berruet.

Nantucket's fine dining scene was relatively small. The Chanticleer existed back then, as it had since 1909, as a simple family place, out in the relatively remote town of Siasconset, or 'Sconset to locals. A group of six or seven investors, all "'Sconseters," had bought the restaurant, in order to keep it from becoming something undesirable to them, like a fast-food joint, but they didn't really have many culinary ambitions beyond that. Nonetheless, they hired Jean-Charles as chef, and after he had proved his intentions, the group sold him the place very reasonably. Thus did Jean-Charles's thirty-year tenure begin.

The Berruets started to improve the offerings slowly because they didn't want to shock anyone. They served cuisine that Jean-Charles calls "Gentle French"—but distinctly upscale from the start. At the beginning, Jean-Charles had to educate his consumers, gradually exposing them to new things, such as sweetbreads and foie gras. But over the years, islanders and tourists grew more sophisticated and well traveled, and they rightly expected the quality to be as good on Nantucket as anywhere in the world. As his audience matured, Jean-Charles began to stretch his wings, until the Chanticleer menu became a full-fledged expression of high-caliber French cuisine.

The art of this cuisine is a passion for Jean-Charles, and his love is apparent in everything on the menu, from the exquisite salad of leeks, tomatoes, basil, and red onions, in which the varied flavors of the vegetables are harmonized by a walnut-oil vinaigrette, to his signature foie-gras terrine. Traditional French entrées such as duck confit are prepared with a sure hand, and succulent local lobsters benefit from a French presentation with sautéed mushrooms and a light curry sauce, served in a delicate pastry shell. Jean-Charles relies upon a single small cheese producer in France to stock his kitchen and create the marvelously balanced cheese tray. As for the wines, the Chanticleer boasts one of the best Burgundy lists in the country, and at almost 40,000 bottles (some 1,200 listings) the restaurant has run out of cellar space.

This font of gourmet artistry is enchantingly housed. The ivy-covered restaurant is tucked discreetly behind a privet hedge. To enter, you must pass through a rose-covered arched white wooden gate into the courtyard, where a colorful antique carousel pony stands guard over an exquisite flower garden. The building itself is classic 'Sconset, with scores of pink roses rambling over sloping roofs. Inside, the feeling is distinctly French as tuxedoed waiters carry custom-made Limoges china to tables with the slight air of snobbery that has always been the epitome of fine French service.

When you first enter the restaurant, you are greeted by Anne, who knows all of the customers and is a gracious and charming host and restaurant manager. Back in the kitchen, Jean-Charles fluidly bops back and forth from English to French, depending on who he is talking to. There is a sense of order amid the great clutter of steaming copper pans. Also in the kitchen are Jean-Charles's sous-chef and right-hand man, Bill Von Ahnen, a two-decade veteran, and his wife, Jackie, who is the pastry chef.

A chef with Jean-Charles's credentials and talent could have a restaurant anywhere in the world, but Jean-Charles prefers things just as they are. His philosophy is timeless. "I go to work every morning with a smile," he has said on more than one occasion, "open the kitchen door, and I'm happy. Some people don't know what happiness is . . . they think it's always better to go a step further. But sometimes, it's better to take a step back. Like with food . . . instead of adding an ingredient to make something better, sometimes you must take away an ingredient. Keep it simple."

Although not many other chefs would call running a restaurant such as the Chanticleer simple, not many other chefs have had the wealth of experience and lucky twists of fate that Jean-Charles has. Of all the places in the world, and of all the great restaurants in the United States, Jean-Charles ended up here—all thanks to Mr. MacAusland and a copy of *Gourmet* magazine!

MENU

Tarte au Foie Gras et Munster Géromé

Turbot avec Marmelade d'Oignon au Cidre

Selle d'Agneau Rôti aux Epices avec Gratin
Dauphinois et Ratatouille Niçoise

Soufflé au Chocolat avec
Sauce au Chocolat

Tarte au Foie Gras
et Munster Géromé

This is a typical Alsatian dish. At the Chanticleer it is served on plates that were made specially for the restaurant by Régis Dho for Philippe Deshoulières Porcelaine de Limoges.

Serves 4

3 tablespoons unsalted butter

3 medium white onions, thinly sliced

Salt and freshly ground black pepper, to taste

4 large fingerling potatoes, scrubbed

1 sheet frozen puff pastry (about 8 ounces), thawed

1/4 teaspoon ground cumin

12 ounces Muenster cheese, rind removed, thinly sliced

4 ounces foie gras, sliced in half, veins removed with a small knife

2 tablespoons sherry vinegar

1 tablespoon walnut or truffle oil

1/8 teaspoon sugar

Minced fresh chives, for garnish

1. Preheat the oven to 375°F. In a skillet over medium-low heat, melt the butter. Add the onions, lower the heat, and cook slowly for 30 minutes, stirring occasionally, until the onions are thoroughly limp and translucent. Season with salt and pepper.

2. Meanwhile, put the fingerlings into a small baking dish and roast for 15 to 20 minutes, until they can be pierced with a sharp knife but are still firm. Let cool, then peel and slice into thin rounds.

3. Increase the oven temperature to 400°F. On a floured surface, roll the puff pastry 3/8 inch thick. Press the puff pastry into an 8-inch tart pan and trim any excess dough; prick all over with a fork. Cover with a layer of potato slices and sprinkle with cumin, salt, and pepper. Top with the sautéed onions and Muenster slices and sprinkle with more pepper. Press down to compact. Bake for 15 to 25 minutes.

4. While the tart bakes, heat a skillet over high heat. Sauté the foie gras in the hot dry pan for 15 to 20 seconds per side, or until barely browned. Top the cooked tart with the foie gras slices and return it to the oven for 1 to 2 minutes.

5. In a small bowl, whisk together the vinegar, oil, and sugar. Brush the tart with this vinaigrette, garnish with the chives, and serve.

Turbot avec Marmelade d'Oignon au Cidre

This delightful dish hails from Normandy, where people cook as often with the local apple cider as they do with wine.

Serves 4

1 cup (2 sticks) plus 1 tablespoon
  unsalted butter, cubed
2 tablespoons extra-virgin olive oil
2 medium white onions, thinly sliced
½ red onion, thinly sliced
1½ cups cider vinegar

2 tablespoons sugar
1½ cups apple cider
3 pounds turbot fillets, skin on
  Salt and freshly ground black pepper,
  to taste

1. In a large sauté pan, heat 1 tablespoon of the butter and 1 tablespoon of the olive oil over medium-low heat. Add the onions and cook, stirring from time to time, until they are translucent and soft, about 5 minutes. Add 1 cup of the cider vinegar and the sugar. Simmer over medium heat until the liquid has evaporated, about 10 minutes. Add 1 cup of the cider and continue to cook, stirring, until the onions are golden and very soft, about 35 minutes.

2. In a small pan over medium heat, combine the remaining ½ cup vinegar and ½ cup cider. Simmer until the mixture is reduced by half, about 7 minutes. Remove the pan from the heat and whisk in the remaining cup of butter, piece by piece. Return the pan to the stove briefly, if necessary, to melt all the butter. The sauce should be thick and satiny.

3. In a nonstick sauté pan, heat the remaining tablespoon of olive oil over medium-high heat. Season the fish with salt and pepper. Place the fish, skin side down, in the pan and cook for 4 to 5 minutes. Turn and cook for 2 to 3 minutes more, until the flesh is opaque.

4. To serve, put the onions in the center of the plate, place the fish on top, and drizzle the sauce over all.

Selle d'Agneau Rôti aux Epices avec Gratin Dauphinois et Ratatouille Niçoise

Serves 4 to 6

FOR THE RATATOUILLE

1 large, ripe tomato

3 tablespoons extra-virgin olive oil

1 medium onion, chopped

½ eggplant, peeled and cut into 1-inch cubes

1 small zucchini, cut into 1-inch cubes

1 red bell pepper, roasted, peeled, and diced (see sidebar, page 148)

1 green bell pepper, roasted, peeled, and diced (see sidebar, page 148)

2 garlic cloves, chopped

Pinch of herbes de Provence

Salt and freshly ground black pepper, to taste

FOR THE GRATIN

1 garlic clove, chopped, plus 1 clove, halved

1 cup heavy cream

3 large eggs

⅛ teaspoon freshly grated nutmeg

Salt and freshly ground black pepper, to taste

3 large baking potatoes, peeled and thinly sliced lengthwise

4 ounces Gruyère cheese, grated (about 1 cup)

FOR THE LAMB

4 garlic cloves, chopped

6 fresh basil leaves

4 fresh sage leaves

2 sprigs of fresh rosemary

Zest of 1 lemon

2 whole star anise, ground

½ teaspoon ground ginger

½ teaspoon ground cinnamon

½ teaspoon ground coriander

Salt and freshly ground black pepper, to taste

Two 14-ounce trimmed boneless lamb loins

2 large pieces caul fat, enough to wrap each loin in

2 tablespoons olive oil

1. To prepare the ratatouille, bring a small saucepan of water to a boil. Fill a bowl with ice water. Plunge the tomato into the boiling water for 30 seconds, then transfer it to the ice water. When it is cool enough to handle, peel and core the tomato with a paring knife, then cut it in half and scoop out the seeds. Dice the tomato into ½-inch cubes.

2. In a medium sauté pan, heat the oil over medium-high heat. Add the onion and sauté for 5 minutes. Add the eggplant and let cook, shaking the pan occasionally, for about 3 minutes. Add the zucchini and cook, gently shaking the pan, for another 2 to 3 minutes. Add the tomato, peppers, and garlic and cook, stirring gently, until the garlic is fragrant, about 2 minutes longer. Add the herbes de Provence, salt, and pepper and cook another 5 minutes. Do not let the vegetables get mushy. They should retain their shape.

3. To prepare the gratin, preheat the oven to 300°F. Spray a 10-inch cake pan with non-stick cooking spray, line the bottom with parchment paper, and rub the parchment and sides of the pan with the cut sides of the halved garlic clove.

4. In a bowl, combine the chopped garlic, cream, eggs, nutmeg, salt, and pepper. Layer the potatoes in the pan tightly, sprinkling all but 2 tablespoons of the cheese between the layers, and packing them down with a spatula. Pour the cream mixture over the potatoes. Sprinkle the remaining cheese on top and bake, uncovered, for 1½ hours, or until firm and browned. The liquid should be absorbed and the potatoes tender.

5. To prepare the lamb, preheat the oven to 450°F. In a blender or food processor, combine the garlic, basil, sage, rosemary, lemon zest, star anise, ginger, cinnamon, coriander, salt, and pepper, and process to a paste. Pat the spice mixture onto both sides of the loins, about 1 tablespoon per side. Wrap the loins in the caul fat.

6. In an ovenproof sauté pan, heat the olive oil over medium-high heat. Cook the loins for 1 to 2 minutes per side, until they are golden brown. Transfer the pan to the preheated oven and roast for 10 to 15 minutes (12 minutes for rare/medium-rare). Remove from the oven and let rest for 5 minutes.

7. To serve, slice the lamb on the bias. Fan the slices on a plate and serve with the gratin and the ratatouille.

Soufflé au Chocolat avec Sauce au Chocolat

This is a very sturdy soufflé. You don't have to worry about it falling—even if you open and close the oven door, jump around, and make noise. The chocolate base can be made through step 3 up to three days in advance. Wrap it tightly in plastic and refrigerate until you're ready to continue. It should be brought back to a warm, but not hot, temperature before you continue with the fourth step.

Serves 8

FOR THE SOUFFLÉ

- 1 cup milk
- 2¼ ounces bittersweet chocolate such as Callebaut, roughly chopped
- 3 large egg yolks
- ⅓ cup plus a pinch of sugar, plus additional for the ramekins
- 2 tablespoons all-purpose flour
- 2 tablespoons melted butter, for the ramekins
- 7 large egg whites

FOR THE SAUCE

- 4 ounces bittersweet chocolate, chopped
- ¾ cup heavy cream
- 2 teaspoons chocolate liqueur, optional

1. To make the soufflé, in a medium saucepan over low heat, stir the milk and chocolate until thoroughly melted and combined.
2. Meanwhile, in the bowl of an electric mixer fitted with the whisk attachment, beat the egg yolks for 10 seconds. Add the ⅓ cup of sugar and beat on high speed until the mixture is pale and light and forms very thick ribbons, 1 to 2 minutes. Reduce the speed to low and add the flour, so that it is evenly incorporated.
3. Add ½ cup of the chocolate mixture to the batter, whisking constantly until combined. Then pour the batter into the remaining chocolate mixture, whisking well. Return to the stove over medium-high heat, whisking constantly and scraping the bottom, for 1½ minutes. The batter will start to pull away from the bottom of the pan

and get very stiff. Let the batter cool, then either use immediately or cover and keep at room temperature for up to 4 hours. You can also chill the batter for up to 3 days; let it come to a warm room temperature before proceeding with the recipe.

4. Preheat the oven to 375°F. Butter eight 6-ounce ramekins and dust them with sugar, tapping out any excess.

5. Whip the egg whites to stiff peaks, adding the pinch of sugar at the end. Whisk about one eighth of the whites into the batter to lighten the mixture. Fold the remaining whites into the batter, a little at a time, folding gently until well incorporated. Fill each soufflé cup almost to the rim and bake for 12 to 15 minutes, or until the soufflés are puffed and have risen above the rims.

6. Meanwhile, prepare the sauce. Place the chocolate in a heat-proof bowl. In a saucepan, heat the cream over medium heat until almost boiling. Pour over the chocolate and stir until melted and smooth. Stir in the liqueur.

7. Serve each soufflé with a little of the chocolate sauce either on the side or poured into a hole in the center of the soufflé.

CIOPPINO'S

20 BROAD STREET

508-228-4622

WWW.CIOPPINOS.COM

SEASON: MAY THROUGH OCTOBER

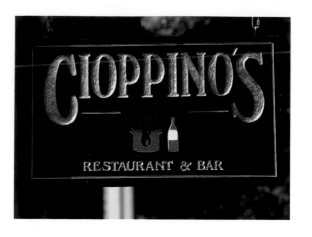

There is a charming tale about how cioppino—that lusty San Franciscan seafood stew—got its name. According to legend, in the seafaring, primarily Italian community of the San Francisco Bay area during the 1930s, the sailors and fishermen would usually eat a huge communal dinner. After being at sea all day, the men would draw straws to see whose responsibility it would be to cook supper on shore in the big iron pot. That person would then go around from boat to boat, collecting ingredients for the evening's stew: a handful of fresh clams, a few wriggling eels, a giant Dungeness crab—whatever the boats had caught during the day. Everyone who ate would "chip in" a little bit, and the steaming seafood mélange made from these chip-ins became known as a cioppino (pronounced *chip*-ino).

Much like the dish after which the restaurant is named, Cioppino's is an eclectic melting pot where diverse, ever-changing elements are harmoniously combined. The menu is based around the seafood-centric cuisine of New England, but the atmosphere has the warm, social feeling of a small-town restaurant on the Mediterranean. With its skylight and breezy ceiling fan, Cioppino's is a nice place to come for lunch. If the weather is lovely, you can dine al fresco on the narrow outdoor patio.

Inside, the small, intimate bar is a focal point of the restaurant. Many a tale is told over that bar, and the wine labels that are encased in resin to create the bar's surface tell a story of their own. The labels are from bottles that the restaurant's owner, Tracy Root, has enjoyed, and they speak of a man who knows and loves wine as much as he knows and loves food, people, and the island.

The restaurant's menu is a melding of familiar dishes with a twist. Tracy recognizes excellent cuisine wherever he encounters it, and on his menu he is willing to cross traditional culinary boundaries. The menu opens with appetizers that cross the flavors of New England and those of the Mediterranean. The clam chowder is brightened with fresh herbs like dill or thyme. The lobster and asparagus salad arrives at the table dressed in a sophisticated lemon-basil vinaigrette. If you're a regular, you can order the fish or pasta every day without eating the same thing twice because the dishes are created nightly, from the day's freshest fish, seafood, and produce.

Of course, the San Francisco cioppino is always on the menu. It is a rich, savory stew of seafood, tomatoes, and wine, served on a bed of linguini. But true to its history, the cioppino is a little different every night, featuring the day's catch, seasoned with the chef's whims. Tracy designed the menu based on the satisfying, straightforward food that his customers want, and a look around the restaurant on a crowded night is all it takes to assure him that he has succeeded.

When Tracy and his wife, Susie, opened Cioppino's in 1991, they set out to create an accessible restaurant that would appeal to a variety of types of people. The place has become an institution for this

reason, and one of its strong points is its awe-inspiring wine list. There are 4,000 bottles in Cioppino's cellar, and 400 wines on the wine list. This list is impressive, but not intimidating, and it's easy to find an affordable bottle of excellent wine, since sixty of the wines are available at less than $30. The selection of California wines is the list's focal point, and it includes seventy-five chardonnays, ninety cabernets, and seventy-five merlots. Then there are the French and Italian wines, the champagnes, and a spectacular reserve list. Tracy is proud to offer a 1970 Haut-Brion at $275, a Sequoia Grove cabernet at $28, and everything in between.

Tracy was born and raised in Connecticut, and he worked in several Connecticut restaurants on his way to deciding that the business could be his career. He traveled to Florida and worked as a maître d' at a restaurant called Daniel's, and it was at this job that he first began learning about wines. Once his interest was piqued, he read voraciously on the subject, and when he was offered a position as maître d' at Nantucket's illustrious Chanticleer in 1979, he realized that this would be an ideal next step in his education.

Jean-Charles Berruet, the Chanticleer's

Tracy and Susie Root.

chef and owner, became Tracy's oenophilic mentor. Together they traveled to France to visit Champagne, Burgundy, and Bordeaux, and Tracy delighted in the wines he had the opportunity to taste, the majestic beauty of the vineyards, and the specialized knowledge he was gaining. In 1985 he went to l'Académie du Vin in Paris and earned his sommelier's certificate. By then, he had developed a pattern of summers on Nantucket and winters in Naples, Florida, where he worked at a restaurant called Margaux. It was in Naples that Tracy met Susie, and they married there in 1985. The ambitious couple decided to start their own Nantucket restaurant, but as it turned out, the restaurant practically fell in their laps.

In 1991 the owner of the building at 20 Broad Street actually asked Susie and Tracy to take the property over, since he knew they had the knowledge and following to make it work. So they renovated the place, built the patio, and opened for lunch and dinner, six days a week. The two have been in the restaurant, from May through October, ever since. They are there all of the time because they love the place, and because it is part of their outlook to be involved in every aspect of the business, from designing the menu to wiping down the tables. Nine times out of ten, if you call Cioppino's, it's Tracy who answers the phone, ready to take a reservation. Susie has a head for business

and she manages all the accounting and paperwork aspects, while Tracy is out on the floor, wearing a kitchen apron to symbolize that he is just as ready to refill a water glass as he is to oversee the service, or to schmooze at the bar.

Tracy is a product of the people he's met, the places he's been, and the foods and wines he has tasted, and this is what makes Cioppino's so personal. Rarely is a person able to express himself as completely in one endeavor as Tracy has. He and Susie run the place with great pride, and loyal customers come back again and again, to see what they're throwing into the pot at Cioppino's tonight.

MENU

Green Tomato Soup
with Chipotle Corn Cream

Roasted Quail Stuffed
with Gorgonzola and
Sweet Italian Sausage

Cioppino's Cioppino

Orange-Cranberry Tart
with Honey–Star Anise Crème Anglaise

Green Tomato Soup
with Chipotle Corn Cream

Make this tangy soup in autumn, when there's a surfeit of fat green tomatoes on the vine. Be sure to wear gloves when handling the chipotle peppers.

Serves 6 to 8

3 tablespoons olive oil

6 large green tomatoes (about 4 pounds), halved and seeded

1 white onion, chopped

¼ cup flour

8½ cups chicken broth, plus more if needed

1 tablespoon sugar

Salt and white pepper, to taste

½ cup half-and-half

1 dried chipotle pepper

1 cup fresh corn kernels (from about 2 small ears corn)

3 tablespoons chopped fresh cilantro

1. In a large soup pot, heat 2 tablespoons of the oil over medium-high heat. Add the tomatoes and onion and cook, stirring, for 5 minutes, or until softened. Stir in the flour and cook, stirring, until the flour turns pale beige, about 5 minutes. Add 8 cups of the chicken broth and simmer the mixture for about 1 hour, stirring occasionally. Season with the sugar and salt and pepper.

2. Strain the soup through a fine sieve, then return the liquid to the pot. Purée the solids in a blender until smooth, then return to the pot. Add the half-and-half and more salt and pepper if necessary.

3. In a hot, dry skillet, char the chipotle on all sides until fragrant, about 1 to 2 minutes. When cool enough to handle, seed, stem, and finely chop the chipotle.

4. In a medium saucepan, heat the remaining tablespoon of oil over medium-high heat. Add the corn and sauté for 2 minutes. Add the remaining chicken broth and simmer until the corn is tender, about 10 minutes. Strain the corn, reserving the stock.

5. In a food processor or blender, purée the corn, adding more broth if necessary to produce a smooth paste. Season with salt and pepper. Strain the purée through a fine sieve, and stir in the chipotle and cilantro.

6. To serve, gently reheat the soup. Ladle it into bowls and drizzle the corn cream on top.

Roasted Quail Stuffed with Gorgonzola and Sweet Italian Sausage

Serves 4

¼ cup pear nectar

2 tablespoons rice wine vinegar

¼ vanilla bean, split and seeds scraped

½ teaspoon vanilla extract

Salt and white pepper, to taste

2 tablespoons olive oil

FOR THE QUAIL

4 semi-boneless quail (4 ounces each)

⅛ teaspoon ground cumin

Pinch of chili powder

Salt and white pepper, to taste

2 tablespoons olive oil

2 cups shiitake mushrooms, cleaned and sliced

¼ pound sweet Italian sausage meat, casings removed and meat crumbled

½ cup crumbled Gorgonzola, plus additional for garnish

2 tablespoons chopped fresh basil

1 quart mixed salad greens

8 cherry tomatoes, preferably a mixture of red and yellow

Pear slices, for garnish

1. To make the vinaigrette, in a small bowl, whisk together the pear nectar, vinegar, vanilla seeds, vanilla extract, and a pinch of salt and pepper. Slowly drizzle in the oil while whisking, then add more salt and pepper to taste. Let the vinaigrette sit at room temperature to develop flavors for at least 1 hour, or refrigerate for up to 2 days.

2. To make the quail, preheat the oven to 400°F. Heat a grill or grill pan to very hot. Season the quail with the cumin, chili powder, salt, and pepper. Place the quail on the grill and sear quickly on all sides to mark. Transfer to a plate to cool.

3. In a medium skillet, heat the olive oil over high heat. Add the mushrooms and crumbled sausage meat and sauté until the sausage is cooked through, about 5 minutes. Turn off the heat and let cool.

CIOPPINO'S

4. In a medium bowl, blend together the sausage mixture, Gorgonzola, and basil. Using a pastry bag with no tip or a spoon, fill the cavity of each bird with about ¼ to ⅓ cup of the mixture. Arrange the quail in a roasting pan and roast for 10 to 12 minutes, or until golden brown and firm to the touch.

5. To serve, toss the greens with enough dressing just to coat them, then divide them among four plates. Top each with a quail, and garnish with cherry tomatoes, Gorgonzola, and sliced pear.

Cioppino's Cioppino

A lemon-scented aïoli brings a piquant touch to this hearty seafood stew.

Serves 4

FOR THE LEMON AÏOLI TOASTS

1 head of garlic

1 cup plus 1 tablespoon olive oil

2 egg yolks

1 tablespoon fresh lemon juice

1 tablespoon cider vinegar

Salt and white pepper, to taste

4 slices baguette bread, toasted

FOR THE CIOPPINO

3 tablespoons olive oil

1/3 cup large-diced yellow bell pepper

1/3 cup large-diced green bell pepper

1/3 cup large-diced red bell pepper

1/2 small onion, diced

1 small leek, white part only, washed well and sliced

2 teaspoons chopped garlic

1 1/2 cups clam juice

1 1/2 cups V-8 juice

3/4 cup canned tomatoes, chopped, juices reserved

1/4 cup red wine

1/4 teaspoon red pepper flakes

1/4 teaspoon Worcestershire sauce

1 teaspoon tomato paste

2 dashes Tabasco, or to taste

2 teaspoons fresh lemon juice

Salt and freshly ground black pepper, to taste

16 mussels, rinsed

8 clams, scrubbed

8 sea scallops

8 shrimp, shelled and deveined

1/4 cup white wine

4 cooked lobster tails, split in half

1 pound cooked pasta (egg, spinach, or tomato linguine or fettuccine)

Chopped fresh basil, flat-leaf parsley, and oregano for garnish

1. To make the aïoli toasts, preheat the oven to 400°F. Cut the top inch off the garlic head and drizzle with 1 tablespoon of the olive oil. Wrap in foil and roast until the garlic is soft, about 45 minutes. When cool enough to handle, squeeze the roasted garlic from the cloves. Set aside.

2. In a blender, combine the egg yolks, lemon juice, cider vinegar, and a pinch of salt and white pepper and blend for 1 minute. With the motor running, slowly drizzle in the

remaining cup of olive oil. Taste and add more salt and pepper if necessary. The aïoli and the roasted garlic will keep for 3 days in the refrigerator.

3. To make the cioppino, in a large, deep-sided pot, heat 2 tablespoons of the olive oil over medium-high heat. Add the peppers, onion, leek, and 1 teaspoon of the garlic and sauté until the vegetables are tender, about 10 minutes. Add the clam juice, V-8 juice, chopped tomatoes and their juices, red wine, pepper flakes, Worcestershire sauce, tomato paste, and Tabasco and bring to a boil. Simmer the mixture until the tomatoes begin to break down, about 15 to 20 minutes. Stir in the lemon juice and salt and pepper and simmer for 5 minutes longer. This part of the stew can be made the day before and kept in the refrigerator.

4. In a large sauté pan, heat the remaining tablespoon of olive oil over high heat. Add the mussels, clams, scallops, and shrimp and sauté for 1 minute. Add the remaining teaspoon of garlic and cook, stirring, until the garlic is fragrant, about 1 minute. Add the white wine, the tomato mixture, and the lobster, and simmer until the shellfish opens, about 3 minutes.

5. Spread the baguette toasts with the roasted garlic, then top with the aïoli. Serve the cioppino over the cooked pasta, garnished with the chopped herbs and aïoli toasts.

Orange-Cranberry Tart with Honey–Star Anise Crème Anglaise

This homey custard tart is paired with a sophisticated sauce flavored with honey and star anise. If the dried cranberries aren't moist and plump, soak them in boiling water for two minutes to rehydrate them.

Serves 8 to 10

FOR THE TART CRUST

1 large egg yolk

2 to 3 tablespoons milk

1¼ cups flour

¼ teaspoon salt

1 tablespoon sugar

8 tablespoons (1 stick) unsalted butter, cut into cubes

FOR THE PASTRY CREAM

½ cup sugar

1 tablespoon cornstarch

1 cup milk

3 egg yolks

2 tablespoons frozen orange juice concentrate

½ vanilla bean, split and seeds scraped, pod reserved for sauce

½ cup dried cranberries

Orange sections, for garnish

FOR THE HONEY–STAR ANISE SAUCE

2 cups milk

½ vanilla bean pod (no seeds)

6 egg yolks

½ cup sugar

3 tablespoons honey

4 whole star anise, ground

1. To make the tart crust, in a small bowl, whisk together the egg yolk and 2 tablespoons of the milk. In the bowl of a food processor, combine the flour, salt, and sugar and pulse 2 or 3 times to combine. Add the butter and pulse to combine. Continue pulsing until the mixture resembles coarse meal. With the motor running, add the egg yolk

mixture through the feed tube, adding the remaining tablespoon of milk if the dough fails to come together in a mass. Turn the dough out of the processor onto a work surface and form it into a ball. Let sit at room temperature for 1 hour.

2. Preheat the oven to 375°F. With a floured rolling pin on a floured work surface, roll the dough to a 12-inch circle; fit it into a 10-inch tart pan, folding any excess dough back over the inside edges of the crust. Prick the dough all over with a fork. Line the tart shell with foil or parchment paper, fill with pie weights, dried beans, or rice, and bake for 15 minutes. Remove the foil and weights and bake the tart until golden brown, 5 to 10 minutes longer. Transfer to a wire rack to cool.

3. To make the pastry cream, in a small bowl, whisk together the sugar and cornstarch. Add ½ cup of the milk, the yolks, and the orange juice concentrate and whisk until smooth.

4. In a saucepan, bring the remaining ½ cup of milk and the vanilla bean seeds to a boil. Reduce the heat to medium and pour in the yolk mixture, whisking constantly. Cook the custard, stirring, until thick, about 3 minutes. Stir in the cranberries and let cool.

5. Spoon the cooled custard into the tart shell. Chill for at least 2 hours or overnight.

6. To make the sauce, in a medium saucepan, combine the milk and vanilla bean pod and bring to a boil. In a small bowl, whisk together the yolks and sugar. Add about ½ cup of the hot milk slowly to the yolk mixture, whisking constantly. Pour the yolk mixture into the pan with the remaining hot milk and cook over low heat, stirring often, until the sauce is thick enough to coat the back of a wooden spoon. Strain through a fine sieve and let cool. Stir in the honey and ground star anise and chill for at least 1 hour and up to 2 days.

7. To serve, cut the tart into wedges and serve each piece with a spoonful of the sauce and the orange segments if desired.

THE
CLUB CAR

1 MAIN STREET

508-228-1101

WWW.THECLUBCAR.COM

SEASON: MAY THROUGH DECEMBER

If the Club Car's reputation as Nantucket's finest restaurant has yet to reach your ears, then surely the sight of its authentic train car from the old 'Sconset Railroad standing idle on Main Street will at least grab your attention. Linger and listen for the melody of an old familiar show tune, maybe "Mack the Knife," flowing from a rickety upright piano tucked on the far side of the railroad car's lacquered red bar. The low arched ceiling and confined space breeds intimacy among the singing clientele, who are sipping cocktails and awaiting a dining room table to savor the Grey Lady's most established cuisine. This is the Club Car, and for those in the know, the name is often uttered in the same breath as the Four Seasons, Chasen's, or Manhattan's own "21" Club.

This restaurant offers a glimpse of a golden age when you could still call the dishes on a menu by their first names:

Oscar, Véronique, Suzette. To step up into the Club Car is to step into the past, not simply in decor but in the grand attitude of dining instead of merely eating. In contrast to the bar's endearing, cramped space, the adjoining Club Car dining room offers expansive walls of windows and a clear line of sight from table to table—letting food lovers and social butterflies alike see and be seen.

Fine service is paramount at the Club Car—from the presence of a proper and attentive maître d', to waiters in white jackets and bow ties. Each devoted staff member proudly acts as a liaison to the kitchen, presenting each course and answering questions with an unwavering knowledge of its preparation.

Make no mistake, however: the Club Car's first strength is its wonderful cuisine. Chef de cuisine Tom Proch and his crew are under the artful guidance of Michael Shannon, executive chef, owner of the Club Car, and "godfather" of Nantucket's restaurant scene. Should Michael retire in the fall of 2001 as he now plans, he will have spent a full fifty years in the kitchen—a feat and story worthy of its own book. But his tales are of the sort best told in person, made richer by his accented speech and the mischievous sparkle in his eyes when he is describing a juicy part. And one thing you can count on is that there is almost *always* a juicy part.

Michael Shannon grew up in a small sea town on the west coast of Ireland. As a boy, his father would often take him along on business to Dublin, where the two dined sumptuously in the city's best French restaurants, most of which were located in grand hotels. It was in just such a place that Michael got his start at the age of seventeen, as an intern at the Shelbourne Hotel. The owner happened to be a family friend who then helped pave the way for Michael to do a yearlong *stage*, or training period, at the Brasserie Georges in Lyons, France. If the Shelbourne whet his appetite for a career as a chef, France sealed his fate, for he lived with the owners above the restaurant and adjacent brewery, devoting every waking hour to the art of French cooking.

A quest for culinary knowledge led him to successively prestigious restaurant kitchens the world over. In the course of his colorful career, Michael has worked in more top-notch restaurants than many of us will ever eat in, from the Waldorf-Astoria Hotel in New York to Chasen's in Hollywood and Claridge's Hotel in London. He has cooked for the Rat Pack in Lake Tahoe and for Ronald Reagan in Grenada—more than 100 restaurants in all, each imparting some small influence that Michael quickly absorbed before moving on to the next challenge.

It wasn't until he landed in southern Vermont, at the Red Fox near Stratton Mountain, that Shannon first met partners Michael O'Mara and Joe Pantorno. O'Mara persuaded them to come to Nantucket in the early seventies to run the Mad Hatter for a season, then on to the restaurant at the Harbor House in 1976. The three worked well together, Shannon in the kitchen, Joe running things on the floor, and O'Mara behind the scenes. They caught the eye of Walter Beinecke, a prominent Nantucket real-estate holder, who liked what they were doing and thought that his Club Car Restaurant (better known then as Leno's, after its manager) would make a perfect showcase for their impressive talents.

So perfect, in fact, that the Club Car remains a preeminent establishment whose devotees have come to rely on Michael and Tom's decision to adhere to cuisine with classical French roots. For example, the Club Car's roast baby New Zealand rack of lamb, gilded with fresh herbs, a mustard glaze, and minted Madeira sauce, embodies basic wisdom about food in a manner that simply cannot be usurped by new-fangled trends. This is true of all the time-honored

Tom Proch and Michael Shannon.

centuries, evolving in the hands of Europe's and America's great chefs. A constantly updated approach keeps the selections fresh yet rich with a tradition that makes each and every dish taste like the definitive rendition. Old favorites like the Club Car's famous crab cakes are joined by equally reliable newcomers such as an appetizer of broiled sesame eel with sweet potato, scallion, frisée, and pickled ginger. New ingredients and methods are seamlessly woven into the Club Car's repertoire, just as new customers come in and become regulars.

Much of what is updated at the Club Car must be credited to Tom, who grew up in Michael's kitchen. When Tom was hired at the Club Car in 1985, after two years at the Opera House, he was a highly motivated twenty-year-old. Tom shares Michael's belief that to achieve a grounded cuisine, a chef must be firmly rooted in the classical and then evolve his own style.

Tom has a great respect for traditional cooking methods. He reads Escoffier, the densely exhaustive 2,973-recipe French cookbook, just for fun. He takes his legacy very seriously, and Michael knows that when he passes the torch, relinquishing control of stoves he has presided over for a quarter century, his exacting standards will be upheld and the flame will burn brightly in both the kitchen and dining room of the Club Car.

dishes on the menu: swordfish encased in a savory, crumbly crust of roasted almonds and walnuts; veal sweetbreads sautéed in brown butter and balanced with aged balsamic vinegar and veal demi-glace. Even a salad of Nantucket tomatoes is given the benefit of French tradition, paired with mesclun greens and topped by a warm potato and goat cheese roulade.

There is timelessness as well as a sense of history to this magnificent cuisine. These recipes have traveled through decades and

MENU

Cold Nantucket Lobster with
Citrus, Avocado, Mesclun Greens, and
Sweet Corn and Potato Savories

Maryland Crab Cake Club Car
with Mustard Cream Sauce

Grilled Veal Medallions
with Fresh Horseradish Cream
and Poached Oysters

Blueberry and Montrachet Tart

Cold Nantucket Lobster with Citrus, Avocado, Mesclun Greens, and Sweet Corn and Potato Savories

Serves 4

FOR THE LOBSTER

10 ounces lobster meat, from tail and claws of a 1½-pound lobster (see sidebar, page 77)

1 orange

1 lime

1 grapefruit

2 ripe avocados, peeled and pitted

Juice of 1 lemon, strained

Salt and freshly ground black pepper, to taste

FOR THE GREENS

2 tablespoons champagne vinegar

1 tablespoon strained fresh lemon juice

½ tablespoon capers

¾ teaspoon finely chopped shallot

¾ teaspoon Dijon mustard

½ teaspoon finely chopped garlic

1 cup olive oil

Salt and freshly ground black pepper, to taste

1 quart mesclun greens

FOR THE SAVORIES

2 large Yukon Gold potatoes, peeled and grated

Kernels from 2 ears of corn, roughly chopped

Salt and freshly ground black pepper, to taste

Olive oil, for frying

1. Remove the lobster meat from the shells and cut it into ½-inch cubes. Peel, segment, and cut the orange, lime, and grapefruit into ½-inch pieces. Chop one of the avocados into ½-inch pieces. In a bowl, combine the lobster, citrus fruit, and diced avocado.

2. In a blender or food processor, add the remaining avocado, the lemon juice, and salt

and pepper; blend until smooth. Pour the avocado purée on the lobster mixture and gently toss to combine. Set aside.

3. To prepare the vinaigrette, in a blender, combine the vinegar, lemon juice, capers, shallot, mustard, and garlic and blend well. With the motor running, slowly drizzle in the oil. Season with salt and pepper and set aside.

4. Preheat the oven to 200°F. To make the savories, in a bowl, combine the potato and corn and season with salt and pepper. In a large nonstick frying pan, heat 3 tablespoons of olive oil over medium-high heat. Drop heaping tablespoonfuls of the potato mixture into the oil and fry them until golden brown on one side, about 3 minutes, then flip and cook on the other side for another 2 or 3 minutes, adding more oil if necessary. Transfer the savories to a plate lined with paper towels, sprinkle with salt, and place in the oven to keep warm. Repeat with the remaining potato mixture and oil until all the savories are cooked.

5. Toss the mesclun greens with enough vinaigrette to lightly coat the leaves. Place the lobster mixture in the center of the plate and garnish with greens and the savories.

Cooking Lobster

Try to buy a live lobster on the day you are going to cook it and store it in the refrigerator until you are ready to prepare the meal. In a large pot, boil water with a pinch of salt. Plunge the lobster into the boiling water and boil gently for 7 to 10 minutes. Transfer the lobster from the pot before its shell has turned thoroughly red, and let drain until it is cool enough to handle. To remove the tail meat, simply turn the lobster onto its back and slice lengthwise through the thin undershell so that the meat can be cut out. For the claw meat, pull the claws away from the arms, then pull and twist the smaller pincer until it comes off, leaving the meat attached to the rest of the claw. Use a heavy knife to crack the claw the short way at the joint. Continue cracking, then use your fingers to pull the meat out whole.

Maryland Crab Cake Club Car with Mustard Cream Sauce

The secret to the Club Car's famous crab cakes is twofold: use only the best-quality lump crabmeat, and use lots of it. You won't find any fillers like bread or cracker crumbs in these extraordinary cakes; they use a frozen shrimp mousse to bind them. And they absolutely melt in your mouth.

Makes 10 crab cakes

FOR THE CRAB CAKES

8 ounces shrimp, peeled and deveined
1 pound jumbo lump crabmeat (see sidebar, page 79), well drained
2½ tablespoons chopped scallions
1 tablespoon chopped fresh flat-leaf parsley
1 tablespoon strained fresh lemon juice
1¼ teaspoons Dijon mustard
½ teaspoon freshly ground white pepper
½ teaspoon salt
Generous dash of Tabasco sauce
Generous dash of Worcestershire sauce
1 large egg
¾ cup heavy cream
2 to 4 tablespoons clarified butter or flavorless oil, such as grapeseed or canola
1 large ripe tomato, blanched, peeled, seeded, and diced, for garnish (optional)
Sprigs of fresh chervil, for garnish

FOR THE SAUCE

8 tablespoons (1 stick) unsalted butter, cubed and chilled
2 tablespoons chopped shallots
6 sprigs of fresh thyme
⅓ cup white wine
2 tablespoons champagne vinegar
⅔ cup clam juice
½ teaspoon balsamic vinegar, preferably 8 years old
½ cup heavy cream
⅛ teaspoon freshly ground white pepper
Salt, to taste
½ teaspoon Dijon mustard
1 tablespoon strained fresh lemon juice

1. To prepare the crab cake mixture, lay the shrimp out on a baking sheet and freeze for 1 hour so the shrimp are semifrozen and firm but not frozen solid.

2. In a medium bowl, gently mix together the crab, scallions, parsley, lemon juice, mustard, white pepper, salt, Tabasco, and Worcestershire sauce. Set aside.

3. Place the semifrozen shrimp in a food processor and pulse a few times to finely chop. Do not overprocess into a paste. Add the egg and pulse to combine. With the motor running, gradually add the heavy cream, scraping the bowl down with a rubber spatula. Scrape the mousse into a large metal bowl and fold in the crab mixture. Fill another large bowl halfway with ice water. Place the bowl with the crab mixture inside the ice bath, cover with plastic wrap, and refrigerate for at least 1 hour and up to 24 hours.

4. Form the crab mixture into 10 cakes. Place them on a tray lined with waxed paper and chill for at least 1 hour and up to 4 hours.

5. To prepare the sauce, in a large sauté pan, melt 2 tablespoons of the butter over medium-high heat. When the foam subsides, add the shallots and sauté for 2 minutes, until translucent. Add the thyme, white wine, and champagne vinegar and simmer the mixture until thick, about 3 minutes. Add the clam juice and balsamic vinegar and continue to simmer until the sauce is reduced to a syrupy glaze, about 12 minutes. Whisk in the heavy cream, white pepper, and salt and simmer until thick enough to coat the back of a spoon, about 5 minutes. Reduce the heat to low and whisk in the remaining 6 tablespoons of butter, one piece at a time, whisking constantly. Turn off the heat and whisk in the mustard and lemon juice. Strain the sauce through a fine sieve, discarding the solids. The sauce will keep at room temperature for several hours. Just before serving, reheat it very gently, taking care not to let the sauce boil.

6. To cook the crab cakes, preheat the oven to 375°F. Heat 2 tablespoons of the clarified butter or oil in a skillet over medium-high heat. Add a few of the crab cakes to the pan (do not crowd them) and cook for 30 to 60 seconds, until golden brown. Flip the cakes and fry for another 30 seconds. Transfer to a baking pan. Repeat with the remaining

Crabmeat

When you purchase crabmeat, try to find out what exactly you are being sold. Lump crab, also called jumbo or backfin, is the highest grade. If you can find it, choose fresh meat that has not been pasteurized; it will be the most delicately flavored. Generally, look for large chunks and white meat, without a lot of broken shell or cartilage. If you decide to cook crabs and pick the meat out yourself, calculate that Dungeness crab is about 25 percent meat and blue crab is about 15 percent, and multiply accordingly, buying between 4 and 7 pounds of crabs to yield 1 pound of meat. Follow the instructions on page 203 (sidebar for Jonah crabs).

cakes, adding more butter or oil to the pan as you go. When the cakes are all browned, bake them for 5 to 7 minutes, or until just firm in the center.

7. To serve, spoon a little of the warm sauce in the center of the plates. Top with the crab cakes and garnish with the tomato and chervil if desired. Serve at once.

Grilled Veal Medallions
with Fresh Horseradish Cream
and Poached Oysters

The pungent flavor of fresh horseradish elevates this simple dish to the sublime.

Serves 4

FOR THE SAUCE

- 1 tablespoon unsalted butter
- 1 cup peeled and chopped fresh horseradish, plus additional for garnish
- 1½ tablespoons chopped shallot
- 1 tablespoon chopped fresh thyme
- 1 teaspoon chopped garlic
- ½ cup white wine

- 1 tablespoon champagne vinegar
- ½ cup veal or beef stock
- 1½ cups heavy cream
- 2 tablespoons unsalted butter, cut into pieces
- 1 teaspoon strained fresh lemon juice
  Salt and freshly ground black pepper, to taste

FOR THE VEAL

- 2 tablespoons unsalted butter
- 2 pounds spinach, stemmed, washed, and dried
  Salt and freshly ground black pepper, to taste
- 8 veal medallions (about 4 ounces each), pounded to ¼ inch thick

- 2 tablespoons olive oil
- ¾ cup white wine
- 1 shallot, finely chopped
- 12 oysters, opened

1. To prepare the sauce, in a large sauté pan over medium heat, melt the butter. Once the foam subsides, add the horseradish, shallot, thyme, and garlic and cook, stirring occasionally, until very soft and translucent, about 3 to 5 minutes. Add the wine and vinegar and simmer to evaporate the liquids. Add the veal stock and simmer until the mixture is reduced by half, about 5 minutes. Add the cream and continue to simmer

until the mixture is reduced by half, another 5 to 7 minutes. Turn off the heat and whisk in the butter and lemon juice until melted. Season with salt and pepper. Strain through a fine sieve, discard the solids, and set aside.

2. To prepare the veal, in a large sauté pan, melt the butter. Add the spinach, salt, and pepper and sauté until barely wilted, about 2 minutes. Cover the pan to keep the spinach warm.

3. Heat a grill pan over high heat. Brush the veal medallions with the oil and season with salt and pepper. Grill until just done, about 30 seconds per side. Tent with foil to keep warm.

4. In another sauté pan over high heat, combine the wine and shallot and bring to a boil. Add the oysters and cook very gently (remove from the heat if necessary) for about 1 minute, until the sides of the oysters just begin to curl. Remove with a slotted spoon.

5. Gently reheat the sauce over low heat. Mound the spinach on 4 plates. Place 2 medallions of the veal on top of the spinach, top with 3 oysters, and surround with sauce. Garnish with grated horseradish.

Blueberry and Montrachet Tart

The Club Car is fortunate to have much of their baking done by longtime island res-
ident and baker extraordinaire Liz Holland. Here is one of her lovely, summery
tarts. It's a dessert, fruit, and cheese course all in one.

Serves 8

FOR THE DOUGH

- 1⅓ cups all-purpose flour
- 1 tablespoon sugar
- ¼ teaspoon salt
- 8 tablespoons (1 stick) unsalted butter, chilled and cut into pieces

- 2 egg yolks, lightly beaten
- 1 to 3 tablespoons half-and-half or milk

FOR THE FILLING

- 1 pound mild goat cheese (Montrachet is best)
- ⅔ cup sugar
- 3 large eggs

- 1 teaspoon vanilla extract
- 1½ cups fresh blueberries, washed, dried, and picked over

FOR THE GLAZE

- 1 cup fresh or frozen blueberries
- ⅓ cup sugar
- ¾ cup water

- 2 teaspoons cornstarch
- 1 teaspoon strained fresh lemon juice

1. In the bowl of an electric mixer fitted with the paddle attachment, combine the flour, sugar, and salt. Add the butter piece by piece, mixing until the dough resembles coarse crumbs. Add the egg yolks and 1 tablespoon of the half-and-half and mix at the slowest speed until the dough comes together in a mass, adding more half-and-half if necessary. Shape the dough into a ball, flatten it into a disk, wrap well in plastic, and chill in the refrigerator for at least 1 hour or overnight.

2. Roll out the dough to a 12-inch circle; fit it into a 10-inch tart pan, folding any excess dough back into the pan to build up the sides. Prick all over with a fork and place in the freezer to chill for at least 20 minutes.

3. Preheat the oven to 375°F. Place a sheet of foil or parchment in the tart shell and fill with pie weights, dried beans, or rice. Bake for 20 minutes. Remove the foil and weights and bake for 5 to 10 minutes more, until golden. Transfer to a wire rack to cool while preparing the filling.

4. Lower the oven to 350°F. In the bowl of an electric mixer fitted with the paddle attachment, beat the goat cheese and sugar for 5 minutes, scraping down the sides as necessary. Add the eggs one at a time, blending well between each addition. Beat in the vanilla. The mixture should be very smooth.

5. Pour the filling into the tart shell and bake in the middle of the oven for 25 to 30 minutes, until the filling is set. Transfer to a wire rack to cool. Arrange the fresh blueberries in an even layer on top of the tart.

6. To make the glaze, in a saucepan over medium heat, combine the blueberries, sugar, and ½ cup of the water and cook until the berries begin to break down and the mixture gets syrupy, about 10 minutes.

7. Meanwhile, dissolve the cornstarch in the remaining ¼ cup of water. Add the cornstarch mixture to the blueberry syrup and bring to a boil, stirring constantly. Cook, stirring, for 3 minutes. Set aside and let cool slightly. Stir in the lemon juice. Brush the glaze generously over the tart just before serving.

COMPANY OF
THE CAULDRON

5 INDIA STREET

508-228-4016

WWW.COMPANYOFTHECAULDRON.COM

SEASON: MID-MAY THROUGH OCTOBER, THANKSGIVING WEEKEND,
AND THE FIRST TWO WEEKENDS OF DECEMBER

Picture yourself entering a romantic culinary fairy tale that features a dollhouse of a restaurant, filled with flowers, lit by candles, its walls lined with antique ship models and copper pots. A harpist plays serenely in the corner. You are tucked into a beautifully set table, but not bombarded with a menu or recited specials. Indeed, you won't be confronted with any decisions to make, or choices to ponder. Instead, you are simply asked to be a willing guest in the gastronomic care of a handsome chef. The same symphonic and seasonal menu is set for you and your fellow diners and you all share front-row seats at this uniquely Nantucket culinary orchestra.

This is sure to be your experience at Company of the Cauldron. Each night, chef All Kovalencik creates and cooks a multicourse feast. With All at the stove, you can melt into your seat, sip an apéritif, and spy the magic worked nightly in the restaurant's narrow open kitchen. White-clad and gray-bearded, All moves precisely among the simmering pots with a confidence born of his vast experience cooking on Nantucket and elsewhere. His demeanor assures you of a great meal to come.

Owned and operated by All and his wife, Andrea, Company of the Cauldron was named for a Renaissance guild of artists and poets who met to discuss their work over dinner, and the communal atmosphere and intense passion for food that you'll find here fit the allusion. The Cauldron's inspiring nightly menus are posted every week, and your only task is to decide which night to come in—a challenge in itself since each four-course dinner sounds more ingenious than the last.

The feast usually begins with either an elegant soup, such as lobster and white bean bisque delicately flavored by tarragon and truffle oil, or a first course such as penne with shrimp, basil, and fresh tomatoes, enriched by a sauce of walnuts and Gorgonzola cream. A salad course comes next, always featuring crisp local greens. The expertly executed entrées include innovative dishes such as grilled leg of lamb in mild red curry sauce served with fresh mango chutney, ginger fried rice, and roasted garlic asparagus; or tandoori swordfish with lavender-scented rice, spicy broccoli sauté, and pappadums. For the dreamy finale, All creates equally unusual desserts, like pistachio-raspberry cake or ginger scones with strawberry-rhubarb compote —a perfect sendoff into the storybook ending of a starry Nantucket evening.

At Company of the Cauldron, you can be certain that every detail of your dinner has been seen to with care. The same can be said about the enchanting decor. Outside, an oversized copper cauldron hangs over the door in lieu of a sign. Window boxes brim with flowers and you are literally beckoned through the entryway by a fabulous tiered wrought-iron baker's rack layered thematically with vegetables and flora. Once inside, the restaurant's rough-hewn beams, small leaded-glass windowpanes, dark wooden built-in cabinetry, and old-fashioned English furnishings will remind you of an old-time tavern. The forty-five-seat dining room is softly lit and it feels as if it has looked this way since the is-

land's whaling heyday. But, in fact, the restaurant was built as the original home of the Boarding House, which is now located at 12 Federal Street.

Andrea, a stunning woman with fantastically long, curly dark hair, has known some of the same loyal customers since she first began working on Nantucket. She spent nine years waiting tables at the Straight Wharf, under the wing of chef Marian Morash, learning the finer points of service, cultivating her knowledge of wines, and refining her palate.

Although both All and Andrea are tall and commanding, they work in their tiny space with an easy air of proprietorship. As a couple, they seem as wedded to their work and the island as to each other. All has a Nantucket restaurant pedigree that reads like a thirty-year history of the island's restaurant scene. He started out in 1970 as a short-order cook at the Sand Piper Restaurant (then one of only two restaurants on Main Street), where he served deep-fried bluefish, slaw, and chowder to a salty cross-section of the island's year-round residents. It was here that his proper name, Allan, was shortened to All, so that he would not be confused with another Allan on staff.

In 1972 All decided to stick around for

a summer job at the Dockside, located on the water at the bottom of the Straight Wharf. For the next couple of years he focused on learning the ins and outs of chefdom and restaurant management. With every job he took (including stints at the Mad Hatter and India House), he gathered more knowledge and experience, refining and elevating his own style of cooking. At the Ship's Inn, then owned and operated by local fixture John Krebs, All had a crash course in classical French cuisine. But it was in Michael Shannon's kitchen at the Club Car that All learned more than he had in all his other jobs combined. Then as now, the Club Car was one of the finest restaurants in New England. Working side by side with this brilliant, classically European-trained chef was like finishing school for All, who soaked up every ounce of knowledge, professionalism, and creativity that Shannon and the rest of the crew could serve up.

In 1986, All accepted an offer to take over as executive chef of Company of the Cauldron, then owned by Steve McCloughsky and Cathy Melo. All's first challenge was to build up a repertoire of set menus. Thanks to his many years of experience on island and off, he was able to rise to the task with enthusiasm and creativity. Eleven years and hundreds of menus later, Steve offered to sell the business to All and Andrea, and they seized the opportunity to continue the legendary romance of Company of the Cauldron, but with their own personal stamp.

The couple bought a home in 1995 and are now year-round Nantucket residents, though they travel extensively during the off-season. After an intense seven-month season, they enjoy taking a much-deserved break, always returning rejuvenated, bursting with energy and ideas for the new season. Not only does All and Andrea's pride in the restaurant shine through in their energetic attention to detail, but the fresh pride derived from ownership now adds an extra-special layer of commitment and satisfaction to their work.

MENU

Hot-Smoked Salmon Beignets with
Rose Pepper Beurre Blanc and Grilled
Red Endive Garnished with Caviar

Mixed Nantucket Field Greens
with Arugula Oil and
Preserved Lemon Vinaigrette

Ginger-Crusted Rack of Lamb with Plum
and Rhubarb Chutney, Scallion Fried Rice,
Steamed Asparagus, and Golden Beets

Chocolate Ganache and Grilled Fresh Figs
with Candied Pecans and Cinnamon Syrup

Hot-Smoked Salmon Beignets with Rose Pepper Beurre Blanc and Grilled Red Endive Garnished with Caviar

You can buy high-quality hot-smoked salmon at specialty food markets. But, if you're up for the challenge, you can also make it yourself (see sidebar, page 92). Just keep in mind that before smoking the fish, it needs to cure for two days. (Curing draws out the moisture and firms up the flesh so that the fish will be better able to accept the smoke.) The result is most definitely worth the effort.

Serves 4 to 6

FOR THE BEIGNETS

4 slices home-style bread, crusts removed, cubed

2 large eggs

¼ cup heavy cream

1 scallion, washed, trimmed, and chopped

2 teaspoons chopped shallot

2 teaspoons Dijon mustard

1 teaspoon washed, dried, and chopped fresh tarragon

½ teaspoon Old Bay Seasoning

5 dashes of Tabasco sauce

⅛ teaspoon freshly ground black pepper

12 ounces hot-smoked salmon, skin removed

Salt, to taste

1 tablespoon olive oil

2 tablespoons minced shallot

¼ cup rice wine vinegar

1 teaspoon ground or crushed pink
peppercorns

8 tablespoons (1 stick) unsalted butter,
cut into 10 pieces

FOR THE ENDIVE

4 to 6 heads of red or white endive
washed, dried, large outer leaves
removed, quartered lengthwise

Olive oil, for brushing

Salt and freshly ground black pepper,
to taste

Golden and tobiko caviar, for garnish

Oil-cured, pitted black olives, for
garnish

1. Preheat the oven to 400°F.

2. To make the beignet batter, in a bowl combine the bread, eggs, cream, scallion, shallot, mustard, tarragon, Old Bay, Tabasco, and black pepper and whisk well, breaking up the bread. Crumble up the salmon and add it to the batter, blending well. Add salt and pepper.

3. Heat a large sauté pan over high heat, then add the oil. Using 2 large soup spoons, mold the batter into ovals (large quenelles) and drop into the hot oil. Cook for 3 minutes until nicely browned; flip and cook for 3 minutes more. Transfer to a baking pan and place in the oven for 5 minutes.

4. To make the beurre blanc, in a small stainless-steel saucepan, over high heat, combine the shallot, vinegar, and pink pepper. Simmer the mixture until it is syrupy and reduced to approximately 2 tablespoons. Lower the heat and slowly whisk in the butter, one piece at a time. Strain the sauce through a fine sieve, discarding the solids.

5. To make the endive, heat a grill or grill pan. Brush the endive with oil and season with salt and pepper. Grill for 30 seconds on each side.

6. To serve, spoon a pool of beurre blanc onto each plate. Arrange the salmon beignets atop leaves of grilled endive. Garnish with caviar and olives.

COMPANY OF
THE CAULDRON

Hot-Smoked Salmon

Line a baking sheet with plastic wrap and arrange 1 pound of boned salmon fillets, skin side down, on the baking sheet. In a stainless-steel bowl, combine ⅓ cup brown sugar, 2½ tablespoons kosher salt, and 2½ tablespoons chopped chives and/or chive flowers. Press the rub firmly and evenly onto the flesh side of the salmon. Cover tightly with plastic wrap and refrigerate for 48 hours.

To hot-smoke the fish on a barbecue grill, burn charcoal until the coals are glowing, then push the coals to one side and sprinkle a handful of soaked wood chips over them. Place the salmon on the grilling rack, on the side not directly over the coals, cover the barbecue, and monitor by looking through the vents to ensure that the wood is smoking, but not too densely, and that it is not flaming. Allow the fish to smoke for 10 minutes for each inch of thickness, until it looks done when you cut into it; the internal temperature should reach 140°F. If you do not plan to serve the salmon immediately, then the internal temperature of the fish should be kept at 180°F. for 30 minutes. This will allow you to store the fish, well wrapped and refrigerated, for up to a week.

Mixed Nantucket Field Greens with Arugula Oil and Preserved Lemon Vinaigrette

This recipe was developed for a special wine-tasting dinner. A bright salad was needed with minimal acidity so as not to interfere with the wines—and this one's perfect. The lemon oil and arugula oil must be made in advance.

Serves 4 to 6

2 cups extra-virgin olive oil
   Julienned zest of 1 lemon

1 bunch of arugula, washed and dried

1 tablespoon minced shallots

1 tablespoon rice wine vinegar

1 teaspoon Dijon mustard

1 teaspoon washed, dried, and chopped
   fresh rosemary

½ teaspoon grated lemon zest

¼ teaspoon chopped garlic

¼ teaspoon anchovy paste
   Salt, to taste

2 quarts mesclun (field greens), washed
   and dried

1. In a small saucepan over medium-high heat, bring 1 cup of the olive oil to 200°F. (it will be too hot to touch but not yet smoking) and add the julienned lemon zest. Cover the pan, turn off the heat, and let sit for 2 hours. Transfer the oil and zest to a bottle and let sit at room temperature, covered, for at least 2 days. You can then store the lemon oil in the refrigerator for up to 1 week.

2. To make the arugula oil, in a food processor, purée the arugula with the remaining cup of olive oil. Transfer the mixture to a bowl, cover, and let sit overnight in the refrigerator before straining through a fine sieve. Arugula oil will keep for 5 days in the refrigerator.

3. In a bowl, combine the shallots, vinegar, mustard, rosemary, grated lemon zest, garlic, anchovy paste, and salt and whisk to combine. Slowly drizzle in ¼ to ⅓ cup of the lemon oil, whisking constantly to combine the ingredients smoothly.

4. Toss the mesclun with the dressing to taste and mound on each plate. Drizzle with arugula oil and serve.

Ginger-Crusted Rack of Lamb with Plum and Rhubarb Chutney, Scallion Fried Rice, Steamed Asparagus, and Golden Beets

Late summer is your only chance to buy both ripe in-season rhubarb and plums at the same time. But, if you would like to take advantage of spring's first tender rhubarb shoots, you can easily and deliciously substitute pitted prunes for the plums.

Serves 4

FOR THE CHUTNEY

- 1 tablespoon olive oil
- 1 cup diced red onion
- 3/4 cup diced sweet bell peppers, preferably a mix of red and yellow
- 1 cup dark brown sugar
- 3/4 cup balsamic vinegar
- 1 1/2 tablespoons peeled and chopped fresh ginger
- 1/2 teaspoon ground cardamom
- 1/2 teaspoon ground cumin
- 1 1/3 cups diced rhubarb
- 1 cup diced pitted plums
- 1/3 cup peeled and diced Granny Smith apple

FOR THE VEGETABLES

- 2 bunches of small golden beets, well washed and trimmed
- 1 bunch of thin asparagus, trimmed
- 1 teaspoon sesame oil
- 1/2 cup chicken stock

FOR THE LAMB

- 1/3 cup drained pickled ginger
- 3 tablespoons Dijon mustard
- Four 10- or 11-ounce frenched double racks of lamb
- Kosher salt and freshly ground black pepper, to taste

94

2 tablespoons plus 2 teaspoons peanut
oil

¾ teaspoon sesame oil

4 large egg yolks

2 cups cooked white rice, preferably
day-old

4 teaspoons chopped shallot

2 teaspoons chopped garlic

2 tablespoons soy sauce

2 scallions, washed, trimmed, and
chopped

1. To make the chutney, in a medium saucepan over medium-high heat, warm the olive oil. Add the onion and ½ cup of the bell peppers and cook, stirring, for 3 to 4 minutes, until the onion is translucent. Add the sugar, vinegar, ginger, cardamom, and cumin and stir to blend. Allow the mixture to simmer until thick, about 20 minutes. Add 1 cup of the rhubarb and the plums and continue to simmer on low heat, uncovered, for 20 minutes. Add the remaining ¼ cup of bell peppers, the remaining ⅓ cup of rhubarb, and the apple, stir, and cook for another 10 minutes. If necessary, add some water to keep the chutney moist and stir from time to time to keep the bottom from burning. Set aside.

2. To prepare the vegetables, fill two large bowls with ice water. In a large pot of boiling water, cook the beets until they can be easily pierced with a fork, about 20 minutes. Transfer the beets from the pot to one of the bowls of ice water to cool. Next, plunge the asparagus into the boiling water and cook until bright green and crisp-tender, about 3 minutes, then drain and transfer to the other bowl of ice water to stop the cooking process. Drain the asparagus and set aside. After the beets have been in the ice water for 10 minutes, drain and peel them (they should slide readily from their skins). Set aside.

3. To make the lamb, preheat the oven to 425°F. In a food processor, purée the pickled ginger and mustard.

4. Sprinkle the lamb generously with salt and pepper. Coat both sides of the lamb meat with the ginger-mustard purée, place on a cake rack inside a roasting pan (for air circulation), and roast until the internal temperature of the lamb has reached 118°F., about 12 to 14 minutes, for medium-rare meat.

5. To make the eggs for the rice, in a nonstick skillet over medium heat, add 2 teaspoons of the peanut oil, ¼ teaspoon of the sesame oil, and the egg yolks; scramble for 1 to 2 minutes. Set aside.

6. To make the rice, heat a large nonstick sauté pan over high heat. Add 1 tablespoon of the peanut oil and let it heat up for 30 seconds. Stir in 1 cup of the rice, 2 teaspoons of the shallot, 1 teaspoon of the garlic, and ¼ teaspoon of the sesame oil, stirring and flip-

ping the mixture constantly. Add 1 tablespoon of the soy sauce and half the scallions and cook until lightly browned, about 3 minutes longer. Transfer to a dish, tent with foil to keep warm, and repeat the procedure with the remaining ingredients. Toss the eggs with the rice mixture and set aside.

7. Meanwhile, complete the vegetables. In a sauté pan, heat the sesame oil over high heat. Add the beets and asparagus and toss to coat. Pour the chicken stock into the pan and simmer until the stock reduces and coats the vegetables. Set aside.

8. To serve, cut the lamb into 4 double chops and accompany each chop with vegetables, rice, and a spoonful of chutney.

Chocolate Ganache and Grilled Fresh Figs with Candied Pecans and Cinnamon Syrup

Any fresh fruit can be used in place of the grilled figs. Pineapple, strawberries, or similarly strong-flavored fruits make a good substitute. Just cut them in one-inch pieces before grilling so they will cook evenly. The candied pecans may seem like a lot of trouble, but leftovers make an irresistible snack.

Serves 4

6 ounces bittersweet chocolate	1 large cinnamon stick
1 cup heavy cream	1/2 cup pecan halves
1 1/2 tablespoons rum	1 cup confectioners' sugar, sifted
1/4 teaspoon vanilla extract	1 quart peanut oil
2/3 cup light brown sugar	4 figs, halved
1/2 cup water	2 teaspoons olive oil
2 1/2 tablespoons dark corn syrup	Whipped cream, for garnish
1/4 teaspoon balsamic vinegar	Mint sprigs, for garnish

1. To make the ganache, melt 4 ounces of the chocolate in the top of a double boiler over, not touching, simmering water. In a small saucepan over medium heat, bring 1/2 cup of the cream to a simmer. Remove the double boiler top from over the water and stir in the scalded cream. Whisk the mixture until smooth, then blend in the rum and vanilla. Let the ganache cool, then refrigerate, covered, until firm but not hardened, about 1 hour.

2. Transfer the ganache to a large mixing bowl and beat with an electric mixer until light and fluffy. In another bowl, beat the remaining 1/2 cup of cream until it forms soft peaks. Fold the cream into the ganache.

3. Line an 8-inch square pan with parchment paper. Spread the ganache evenly into the pan and freeze, covered, for 1 hour, until firm.

4. In the top of a double boiler over simmering water, melt the remaining 2 ounces of chocolate. Brush the melted chocolate over the ganache, then cut the ganache into diamond shapes immediately. Refrigerate, covered, until ready to use (up to 3 days).

5. To make the cinnamon syrup, in a saucepan over medium heat, combine the brown sugar, water, corn syrup, vinegar, and cinnamon stick and stir until the sugar is dissolved. Raise the heat and bring the liquid to a boil. Cover and cook for 3 minutes. Uncover, and cook until the mixture reaches syrup consistency, about 5 minutes. Strain through a fine sieve, discarding the solids. Set aside.

6. In a pot of boiling water, simmer the pecans for 1 minute. Drain, then toss the blanched pecans with confectioners' sugar, shaking off any excess.

7. In a deep sauté pan or wok, bring the peanut oil to 325°F. Add the pecans and fry for 2 to 3 minutes, stirring occasionally so they don't stick together. Transfer to a plate lined with a paper towel and let cool. The candied pecans can last up to 1 month stored in an airtight container.

8. To make the grilled figs, heat a cast-iron grill until it smokes. Brush the cut side of the figs with the olive oil and grill for 1 minute, then turn and grill for 30 seconds longer.

9. To serve, arrange 3 ganache diamonds, 2 fig halves, and 4 pecans on each dessert plate. Drizzle with cinnamon syrup and garnish with whipped cream and mint sprigs.

DEMARCO

9 INDIA STREET

508-228-1836

WWW.NANTUCKET.NET/FOOD/DEMARCO

SEASON: MID-MAY THROUGH MID-OCTOBER

On a small, delightful island, located many, many miles off the coast of Italy, there is a little restaurant known for its perfectly seasoned, classic Italian food and open, congenial atmosphere. Though this island is really located considerably far from Italy—off Cape Cod, actually—at DeMarco, there is no mistaking where you are.

Just step into this town house turned rustic restaurant and you'll bask in the radiant Italian hospitality. In the main room on the ground level, original wood floors, clean white walls capped with huge, handsome rough-hewn wooden beams, a beautiful round bar, and impressionistic, island-inspired art contribute to the simple, peasantlike Mediterranean appeal. The upstairs dining room is more majestic, with its arching cathedral ceiling that allows for an enormous wooden sculpture winding sinuously from the floor. But on both levels, the wait staff is knowledgeable and warm, and as they guide you through the alluring menu, helping to pair a Tuscan wine with today's freshly caught fish special, you relax, assured that your dining experience is in good hands.

Don DeMarco, the mastermind behind the DeMarco experience, has the quiet, mood-assessing skill of the best hosts. If you are in the mood to chat, Don is even apt to join you at your table. He loves good conversation and possesses a rare vitality and exuberance, whether you care to discuss art, business, food, politics, or tennis. His attitudes toward running a restaurant are apparent in the pleasant and direct way in which you are treated by everyone at De-Marco's. As Don is fond of saying to his staff, "The public will forgive anything but indifference."

Far from indifferent, DeMarco's northern Italian food is excellent, served with enthusiasm and creativity. Don treats Nantucket as if it were anchored in the azure waters of the Mediterranean, featuring just-picked local produce, fresh meat, and an abundance of seafood on the traditional menu. The day's seafood catch is often melded in a rich tomatoey bisque thickened with saffron garlic aïoli. Shrimp might be sautéed in a light, piquant sauce with garlic, white wine, and fresh herbs, served over perfectly cooked angel hair pasta. Savor the braised monkfish, cooked with sundried tomatoes, artichokes, and leeks, served over cauliflower purée in marjoram-scented broth, or choose an equally ethereal and flavorful spring chicken with pearl onions, morel mushrooms, and asparagus over polenta in a Barolo wine sauce.

As you relish the meal, the cozy surroundings, and the lively chatter, you may begin to wonder about the man who makes it all possible. Don, the intensely creative and energetic son of Italian immigrant parents from upstate New York, has always been a people person. In school, and later working on various political campaigns, Don used his talents to rouse enthusiasm and to network. He is perceptive and analytical, which makes him able to identify the perfect kind of person needed for any position. This is also the side of him that hires "people-people who are good, strong, independent thinkers" at the restaurant. He meets with all the staff weekly and makes a point of checking in with everyone informally on a daily basis. This allows him to keep tabs on what people are doing, talk about food trends, know what equipment is needed, while he also makes a point of encouraging each staff member's initiatives. If a server shows interest, Don invites him or her to come in early to do some work in the kitchen, and he always wants to hear new food ideas from the chef and even the dishwasher.

If networking, politics, psychology, and management are part of Don's success, it is his creativity—and his desire to encourage creativity in others—that powers him. He vividly describes an inspiring trip that he took to Greece as a young man, just before he discovered Nantucket. He fell in love with the austere beauty of the Greek islands. Don then flew from Greece

to Nantucket, filled with imagined vistas of the island and determined to expand beyond the one-track business career he had been in.

As his plane approached Nantucket, Don became enamored of the place before the plane even landed. During his first stay, he bought the ramshackle property at 9 India Street. First he renovated from top to bottom, deciding what to do with the space as he went. By the time he was finished, the building had the feel of an elegant country inn—perfectly matched to the refined cuisine of northern Italy that Don had always loved. Next, he set about staffing and decorating the restaurant, and with DeMarco he opened a fresh chapter in his life.

Throwing himself into this new existence, Don became hooked on the restaurant business. He still enjoys his city life in New York, but every summer Don returns to the island to run the restaurant and savor the beauty of Nantucket and to carry on that wonderful, warm Italian tradition of long, relaxed, sociable meals, sitting down to dinner in the restaurant almost every night of the week with his extended "family" —guests, friends, and staff—to enjoy the simple pleasures of great company and marvelous food.

MENU

Oysters with Gazpacho Vinaigrette

■

Beet Ravioli with Truffle Butter Sauce

■

Veal Chops alla Milanese
with Oven-Roasted Tomatoes

■

Panna Cotta with Berries

Oysters with Gazpacho Vinaigrette

Serves 6

2 ounces green beans, cut into 1-inch lengths (about ½ cup)

1 red bell pepper, minced

1 celery stalk, minced

½ medium red onion, minced

½ large cucumber, peeled, halved, seeded, and minced

Juice of 2 limes, strained

2 strips of lime zest (about 1 inch wide each)

1 cup V-8 juice

2 tablespoons extra-virgin olive oil

1 tablespoon chopped fresh cilantro

1 teaspoon red wine vinegar or sherry vinegar

1 teaspoon minced peeled fresh ginger

6 dashes of Tabasco sauce

Salt and freshly ground black pepper, to taste

36 oysters, preferably blue points

Crushed ice or fresh greens, for serving

Lemon wedges, for garnish

1. Fill a bowl with ice water. To blanch the beans, bring a large pot of water to a boil over medium-high heat, add the green beans, and cook until crisp and bright green, 2 to 3 minutes. Drain the beans, then immediately plunge them into ice water to cool. Drain and finely mince.

2. In a bowl, mix together the bell pepper, celery, onion, cucumber, blanched beans, and lime juice and zest and let sit for 2 or 3 minutes.

3. Stir in the V-8, oil, cilantro, vinegar, ginger, Tabasco, salt, and pepper and let sit for at least 30 minutes (or up to 2 days refrigerated).

4. Clean and open the oysters. Arrange them on crushed ice or fresh greens. Sprinkle with freshly ground black pepper and add lemon wedges for garnish. Just before serving, pour 1 teaspoon of the vinaigrette over each oyster.

Beet Ravioli with
Truffle Butter Sauce

This dish combines the earthiness of beets with a warm buttery sauce. The ravioli can be frozen for up to three months. then cooked without defrosting.

Serves 8

½ pound beets (about 3 small). scrubbed and trimmed

4 tablespoons olive oil

3 large Spanish onions. peeled. halved lengthwise. and thinly sliced

1 cup dried, unseasoned breadcrumbs

1 cup grated Parmesan cheese

2 large eggs

½ teaspoon salt, plus additional to taste

¼ teaspoon freshly ground black pepper, plus additional to taste

1 package wonton wrappers (see Note, page 10)

6 tablespoons unsalted butter

1 tablespoon truffle oil

¼ cup finely chopped fresh chives

1. Preheat the oven to 400°F. Bring a large saucepan of water to a boil over high heat. Add the beets and cook, covered, for 30 to 40 minutes, until the beets are tender.

2. Meanwhile, in a large skillet, heat the oil over medium heat. Add the onions and cook, stirring occasionally, until golden brown and caramelized. Once the onions begin to brown, stir frequently so they do not burn. It will take about 25 to 30 minutes.

3. When the beets are done, drain and let cool until you can handle them. Peel and quarter them, then place them on a baking sheet and roast for 5 minutes.

4. In a food processor fitted with the metal blade, add the beets, onions, breadcrumbs, ³/₄ cup of the Parmesan, one of the eggs, and the salt and pepper. Pulse lightly to combine.

5. In a small bowl, lightly beat the second egg. Brush one side of one wonton wrapper with egg and place 1 tablespoon of the beet mixture in a nice mound in the center. Press a second wonton wrapper down gently, tamping down around the filling with the back of a spoon or your finger. Trim the edges of the ravioli with a 3-inch round biscuit cutter. Smooth out any apparent air bubbles before cooking or freezing. Continue with the remaining wonton wrappers and the beet mixture.

DEMARCO

6. To cook the ravioli, bring a large pot of salted water to a boil. Add the ravioli and cook for 4 to 5 minutes, or until the edges are tender. Do not drain.

7. While the ravioli are cooking, make the butter sauce. In a large sauté pan, melt the butter and truffle oil. Stir in 3 tablespoons of the pasta water and the remaining ¼ cup of grated Parmesan and bring to a simmer. Add the chives and salt and pepper to taste. Using a slotted spoon, transfer the ravioli to the sauce in the pan. Stir to coat and serve immediately.

Veal Chops alla Milanese
with Oven-Roasted Tomatoes

This is a wonderfully simple way to enjoy this cut of veal. The veal pan juices mingle with the balsamic vinegar, creating a light but extremely flavorful sauce. And, best of all, it's quick to make.

Serves 6

6 large ripe red tomatoes, halved and seeded
1 cup plus 6 tablespoons olive oil
Salt and freshly ground black pepper, to taste
1 cup balsamic vinegar
Six 12-ounce center-cut veal chops, bone in
4 large eggs
2 tablespoons water

2 cups unseasoned breadcrumbs
12 tablespoons (1½ sticks) unsalted butter
3 bunches of arugula, trimmed, washed, and dried
1 fennel bulb, trimmed and julienned or sliced very thin
Juice of 2 lemons, strained
Parmesan shavings, for garnish

1. Preheat the oven to 450°F. In a roasting pan, arrange the tomato halves, skin side up. Drizzle with 3 tablespoons of the olive oil and season with salt and pepper. Roast for 15 to 20 minutes, until shriveled. Transfer the pan to a wire rack to cool. When the tomatoes are cool enough to handle, peel them over a bowl and squeeze the flesh into chunks. Reserve the tomato flesh and juices.

2. In a small saucepan over medium-high heat, add the vinegar and simmer until reduced to ¼ cup, about 15 minutes. Let cool.

3. Trim the veal chops of excess fat and pound gently to ½ inch thick. In a small bowl, whisk together the eggs and water. Brush the egg wash on both sides of the chops, then evenly press in the breadcrumbs and sprinkle with salt. Divide 1 cup of the olive oil and all of the butter between 2 large, heavy pans over medium-high heat. Let the pans heat until the butter melts and the foam subsides. Add the chops to the pans; the fat should come at least halfway up their sides. Cook the chops until they are golden

brown and crusty on both sides. If the chops cook too quickly the insides won't cook and the outsides will overcook; if they cook too slowly they will "steam" and get soggy. Flip when the chop reaches a rich golden brown, about 6 to 7 minutes. Shake the pans gently from time to time to make sure the chops are not sticking. Do not allow the crust to break. After another 6 or 7 minutes, transfer the chops to plates lined with paper towels and keep warm.

4. In a bowl, combine the roasted tomatoes and their juices, arugula, fennel, lemon juice, remaining 3 tablespoons of olive oil, and salt and pepper; toss well.

5. Mound a portion of the salad in the center of each plate, drizzling the balsamic reduction on top. Top with a chop and garnish with Parmesan shavings.

Panna Cotta with Berries

Cloudlike and wobbly, this lightly sweet pudding is a cooling dessert on a sultry evening.

Serves 6

2 cups heavy cream	½ pint blueberries
⅓ cup plus 2½ tablespoons sugar	½ pint blackberries, halved
1 vanilla bean	8 large strawberries, sliced
2 tablespoons rum	Juice of 1 lemon, strained
1½ tablespoons powdered gelatin	Crushed amaretto cookies, for garnish
½ pint raspberries	

1. In a metal saucepan, combine the cream and ⅓ cup of the sugar. Split the vanilla bean in half lengthwise and scrape the seeds into the pan; add the pod as well. Slowly bring the mixture to a boil over medium-low heat. Remove the pan from the heat and allow to cool.

2. Place the rum in a small saucepan and sprinkle the gelatin on top. Let the mixture sit until the gelatin softens, about 5 minutes. Place the pan over low heat and cook, stirring, until the gelatin dissolves, about 5 minutes. Scrape the gelatin-rum mixture into the cream, whisking to combine. Pour the mixture through a fine sieve and divide it between six 4-ounce ramekins. Chill until the creams are set, about 4 hours or overnight.

3. In a bowl, combine the raspberries, blueberries, blackberries, and strawberries, the remaining 2½ tablespoons of the sugar, and the lemon juice and let sit for 5 minutes.

DEMARCO

4. In a skillet over high heat, sauté the berry mixture for 30 seconds, stirring, then turn off the heat.

5. Run a knife around the edges of the molds and invert each onto a dessert plate, smacking the molds with the palm of your hand if the panna cottas are reluctant to slide out. Spoon the berry mixture around each panna cotta and sprinkle the top of each with crushed amaretto cookies.

THE GALLEY
ON CLIFFSIDE BEACH

JEFFERSON AVENUE

508-228-9641

SEASON: MEMORIAL DAY WEEKEND THROUGH SEPTEMBER

Some Nantucket restaurants, such as the Club Car and the Chanticleer, are most revered for their superior food and service. Others, like 21 Federal and Le Languedoc, thrive on a boisterous and friendly scene as much as fine menus. No Nantucket restaurant, however, can hold a candle to the Galley when it comes to setting. It is the only restaurant on the entire island smack dab on the beach, making it a wildly popular choice for both lunch and dinner. And it is the hottest reservation on island for the Fourth of July, when a few lucky diners can feast decadently in the restaurant while gazing at fireworks exploding brilliantly in front of them on the surrounding beach. Even on a regular summer evening, fashionable clientele have been known to burst into spontaneous applause or snap camera shutters from their coveted reserved tables as the sun sets spectacularly over the Galley's pristine sands.

The Galley is currently managed by a fourth generation of Nantucket restaurateurs. Its humble beginnings reach back to the 1920s, when it began as a lunch shack serving bathers at a public beach. Nearby lockers were used by high-society vacationers who came to the beach to bathe, shedding their fancy dresses, hats, and gloves and walking down to the water in elaborate swimming costumes.

In the 1940s, the Cliffside Beach Club became private, and the Galley continued to serve as a lunch stand for ladies and gents who lounged under the club's signature big beach umbrellas and raised little flags for chaise-side service. Simple island foods such as raw oysters, clams, and sandwiches were nonetheless served elegantly, on china plates carried to the beach on trays.

In 1957, Robert and Emma Lea Currie bought the Cliffside Beach Club, which included the Galley. Robert, a Nantucket native, had grown up spending afternoons at the Gray Gull, a restaurant his parents owned on Liberty Street behind the Methodist church. Back then you could get dinner for a dollar, and a good tip was ten cents. He had worked as a lifeguard at Cliffside in 1934 and had forever dreamed of owning it. Along the way he met Emma Lea, originally from Maryland, when she worked as a waitress for the Curries. They married and, years later, came to run the Galley together. It was Emma who established the tradition of filling an old dory at the restaurant's sandy entrance with flowers. To this day, a steady stream of tourists comes to the Galley to photograph the quaint, geranium-filled boat.

The Galley carried on under the Curries as an open-air restaurant serving lunch exclusively to the members of the private beach club. Jane Silva (née Currie) took the restaurant over from her parents in 1972. A few years later, during a trip to Europe with her partner, Ivan Skender, she became inspired by the flower-filled outdoor cafés of southern France and decided to bring the Côte d'Azur to Nantucket by turning the Galley into a similarly chic public restaurant. She was friendly with Lucien Van Vyve, the Opera House's chef of thirty years, and it was Lucien who taught Jane to cook. She absorbed his repertoire of French rolled omelets and classic salads, which were perfect offerings for the ladies who loved to lunch at the Galley. She also instituted a bevy of changes, adding a dining

room and awnings under which posh luncheons, cocktail parties, and private dinners flourished. By 1979, Jane had turned the Galley into a thriving, popular beachside bistro. Mentor Lucien Van Vyve lives on through his enchanting, risqué line drawings of topless mermaids, which continue to adorn the Galley's walls and wine list.

Jane's handsome sons grew up at the Galley, washing dishes, busing tables, and working every summer throughout college. After graduation, both initially turned elsewhere to seek their fortunes. Geoffrey worked at a hotel in Singapore for two winters, followed by a year as general manager for fine dining at Boston's Hampshire House and then two winters at Café Europa in Palm Beach. Though he might not have been consciously thinking about it at the time, this business and operational experience would prove handy when he and his brother would later come to carry on the family name at the Galley.

David, in turn, went to New York City after college and worked as the sous-chef at MK, a hip club in the 1980s. David enjoyed the creative license and extravagance of the job for a while, but then he decided to leave the East Coast and try his luck out west. He landed at San Francisco's Atrium as manager of special functions before opting to shift gears and run his own landscaping company specializing in Japanese gardening and bonsai.

But both brothers found themselves repeatedly drawn back to Cliffside in the summer. Jane felt that no one else knew or cared about the restaurant as much as they did, and she was grateful for their help. Finally, the two committed to running the restaurant full-time.

Geoffrey and David have made subtle changes and updated the restaurant's menu and wine list, each bringing something different to the mix. Geoffrey's connections in Palm Beach enabled him to recruit staff during the winters, while David planted a wonderful organic chef's garden filled with fruit trees, herbs, a dozen kinds of tomatoes, lettuces, arugula, striped beets, Japanese eggplants, peas, beans, and squash blossoms. As a chef himself, David knows that "the ultimate experience is taking something from seed to plate."

Despite David's proficiency in the kitchen, running the restaurant can be extremely demanding, so the brothers decided to hire an executive chef, someone who could help the Silvas update the menu while keeping the Galley true to its rich history. Now, the menu is classic yet modern, a distinctly summery blend of Nantucket and Riviera flavors. Sitting right by the ocean, in the breezy dining room where white wicker,

chintz, and geraniums set the perfect beach-side mood, it's hard to resist ordering one of the Galley's seafood specialties. Recent menus have included perfectly grilled fresh sea scallops, served with creamy polenta, a peppery pancetta-watercress salad, and a woodsy porcini-thyme nage. It is also great fun to order a simple platter of raw oysters in this airy setting, imagining the elegant ladies and gents of the 1940s indulging in the same delicacy in the very same spot. Should you be in a carnivorous mood, the menu always lists several traditional meat dishes, such as a first-rate osso buco or a Black Angus steak. Whatever one craves, all the food is expertly prepared and professionally presented.

Chatting with the Silva family offers an enlightening education on what it means to be a fourth-generation Nantucket restaurateur. Jane, Geoffrey, and David know the place as only someone who has grown up here can, and the serenity of the beach and the island still entrance them. They will tell you that they wouldn't trade their business for any other in the world, and it's not hard to imagine why. After all, theirs is the most idyllic spot on one of the world's most idyllic islands.

MENU

Nantucket Chowder with Yukon Gold
Potatoes, Applewood-Smoked Bacon,
and Fresh Thyme

Goat-Cheese-Stuffed Squash Blossoms
with Grilled Onion and
Organic Tomato Vinaigrette

Lobster Risotto
with Mushrooms and Asparagus

Rosewater Angel Food Cake
with Blackberries and
Lemon Verbena Syrup

Nantucket Chowder with Yukon Gold Potatoes, Applewood-Smoked Bacon, and Fresh Thyme

A New England classic gets a modern update with this enticing chowder, in which both clams and mussels appear still in their shells.

Serves 4 to 6

10 ounces thick-cut applewood-smoked bacon, diced

6 tablespoons unsalted butter

2 celery stalks, chopped

1 medium onion, chopped

²/₃ cup all-purpose flour

6 cups (or one 46-ounce can) clam juice

1 pound Yukon Gold potatoes, scrubbed and cut into ½-inch dice

20 mussels, scrubbed

8 littleneck clams, scrubbed

8 Manila clams, scrubbed

1 cup heavy cream

2 tablespoons chopped fresh flat-leaf parsley

1 tablespoon chopped fresh thyme
Cracked black pepper, to taste

1. In a large pot over medium-low heat, crisp the bacon with the butter for 5 to 6 minutes. Add the celery and onion and cook for 3 to 4 minutes longer. Add the flour and blend well, cooking until the flour turns pale beige, about 2 minutes. Add the clam juice and bring to a boil. Allow the chowder to reduce and thicken for 2 to 3 minutes. Add the potatoes and simmer over low heat until tender, about 15 minutes. Add the mussels and clams and simmer until the shells open wide, about 2 to 3 minutes.

2. To finish, stir in the cream, parsley, thyme, and pepper. Return briefly to a simmer and serve.

Goat-Cheese-Stuffed Squash Blossoms with Grilled Onion and Organic Tomato Vinaigrette

David grows the squash blossoms and tomatoes himself in the Galley's organic garden.

Serves 4

8 ounces mild goat cheese

1 teaspoon chopped fresh thyme

1 teaspoon chopped fresh rosemary

1 teaspoon chopped fresh tarragon
  Pinch of red pepper flakes

3/4 cup extra-virgin olive oil, plus additional for the onion and bread slices

1/4 cup balsamic vinegar

1 tablespoon chopped fresh flat-leaf parsley
  Salt and freshly ground black pepper, to taste

1 medium red onion, cut into 1/2-inch slices

1 organic ripe tomato, seeded and chopped

6 arugula leaves, chopped

4 sprigs of fresh opal basil, chopped

4 slices of sourdough bread

2 large eggs

3/4 cup all-purpose flour

4 large squash blossoms

1. In the bowl of an electric mixer fitted with the paddle attachment, beat the goat cheese, thyme, rosemary, tarragon, and red pepper flakes on high speed. Place the cheese mixture in a pastry bag with no tip and set aside. (Alternately, place the cheese mixture in a heavy-duty plastic bag and cut a small hole in one corner.)

2. In a small bowl, whisk together 1/2 cup of the olive oil with the vinegar, parsley, salt, and pepper. Set aside.

3. Brush the red onion slices with olive oil. In a grill pan over high heat, cook the slices

until softened, about 3 minutes per side. Remove from the heat, allow to cool slightly, and chop.

4. In a large bowl, toss the grilled onion, tomato, arugula, and basil with the vinaigrette.

5. Brush each slice of bread with olive oil. Place the slices on the grill pan and grill until golden brown, about 2 minutes per side.

6. In a shallow dish, beat the eggs with salt and pepper. On another plate, toss the flour with salt and pepper. Remove the pistils from the squash blossoms. Put the pastry bag all the way into each squash blossom and gently fill with the cheese mixture, taking care that the petals don't separate too much. Coat the blossoms thoroughly with egg, then dip them in the flour.

7. Add the remaining ¼ cup of oil to a large sauté pan and heat over medium-high heat for 45 seconds. Fry the blossoms for 15 seconds on each side, transferring them to a plate lined with a paper towel as they finish cooking.

8. To serve, place the blossoms on plates, spoon some vinaigrette on top, and serve each with a slice of grilled sourdough bread.

Lobster Risotto with Mushrooms and Asparagus

Serves 4

FOR THE LOBSTER BROTH

2 tablespoons olive oil

1 large onion, cut into chunks

2 celery stalks, cut into chunks

1 carrot, cut into chunks

2 medium leeks, whites only, well
washed and cut into chunks

6 garlic cloves, peeled

8 cups water

1 cup white wine

1/4 cup tomato paste

1 generous bunch of fresh thyme sprigs

3 bay leaves

1 teaspoon whole peppercorns

Two 1 1/2-pound lobsters

FOR THE RISOTTO

1/4 cup plus 2 tablespoons olive oil

1 small onion, chopped

2 cups arborio rice

2 cups white wine

4 1/2 cups lobster broth, warmed

10 tablespoons (1 stick plus 2
tablespoons) unsalted butter

1/2 cup grated Parmesan cheese

1/2 cup grated Asiago cheese

1 teaspoon salt

3 to 4 ounces mushrooms, cleaned and
sliced thickly

1 bunch of thin asparagus, trimmed to
leave 3-inch tips

1 tablespoon chopped fresh thyme

1 tablespoon chopped fresh flat-leaf
parsley, plus additional as garnish

1. To prepare the lobster broth, in a stockpot large enough to accommodate 2 lobsters, heat the oil over medium-high heat and add the onion, celery, carrot, leeks, and garlic. Cook until the onion begins to soften, about 3 minutes. Add the water, wine, tomato paste, thyme, bay leaves, and peppercorns and bring to a boil. Simmer for 10 minutes. Add the lobsters and return to a boil. Cook, partially covered, for 9 minutes. Remove the lobsters and set aside. Strain and reserve the cooking liquid. The broth can be made up to 3 days in advance and stored in the refrigerator. Reheat before preparing the risotto.

2. Remove the lobster meat from the tail and claws, keeping it whole if possible (see sidebar, page 77). Slice the lobster tails crosswise into 4 pieces and reserve the whole claws.

3. To prepare the risotto, in a large, heavy-bottomed saucepan, heat ¼ cup of the oil over high heat. Add the onion and sauté for 1 minute. Add the rice and sauté for 2 minutes longer. Add the wine and reduce the heat slightly. Simmer and stir until all the wine has evaporated, about 5 minutes. Add 1 cup of the broth and cook for about 5 minutes, stirring occasionally to ensure that the risotto is not sticking to the pan. When the first cup of broth has been absorbed by the rice, add another cup and cook, stirring, for 5 more minutes. Repeat with a third cup of broth. When the 3 cups of liquid have been absorbed, stir in 8 tablespoons of the butter, the cheeses, and the salt.

4. To make the sauce, in a sauté pan, heat the remaining 2 tablespoons of oil and 1 tablespoon of the butter over medium-high heat. Add the mushrooms and brown for 1 minute. Add the asparagus and the remaining 1½ cups of lobster broth. Let simmer until reduced by half, about 5 minutes. Add the lobster meat, herbs, and the remaining tablespoon of butter.

5. To serve, spoon the mushroom sauce around a mound of risotto and garnish with parsley.

Rosewater Angel Food Cake with Blackberries and Lemon Verbena Syrup

If you have mini Bundt molds, feel free to use them in place of the large tube pan. It makes a pretty presentation.

Serves 10 to 12

FOR THE CAKE

2 cups egg whites (about 13 whites)

1½ teaspoons cream of tartar

1 tablespoon rosewater (preferably Lebanese "al wadi" brand)

2 teaspoons vanilla

½ teaspoon salt

1¼ cups confectioners' sugar, sifted

1 cup cake flour, sifted

FOR THE SYRUP AND GARNISH

1 cup water

1 cup granulated sugar

10 sprigs of lemon verbena

Whipped cream, for garnish (optional)

Blackberries, for garnish

1. To prepare the cake, preheat the oven to 325°F. In the bowl of an electric mixer fitted with the whisk attachment, beat the egg whites on low speed until frothy. Add the cream of tartar, increase the speed to medium, and whip until soft peaks form. Add the rosewater, vanilla, and salt and mix to combine. Gradually add the sugar and continue to whip on high speed for 3 to 4 minutes, or until stiff peaks form. Gradually fold in the flour in 4 batches. Spoon the batter into a 10-inch tube pan.

2. Bake the cake until a tester inserted near the middle comes out clean, about 50 to 60 minutes. Cool the cake upside down (over a wine bottle works well) before unmolding.

3. To prepare the syrup, in a saucepan, combine the water and sugar and boil for 2 minutes. Let cool completely.

4. Bring a small saucepan of water to a boil. Fill a bowl with ice water. Place the lemon

verbena in a strainer and lower it into the boiling water to blanch for 30 seconds. Transfer the strainer to the ice water to cool. Shake off excess water from the verbena and pinch off the leaves from the sprigs. In a food processor or blender, purée the verbena with the sugar syrup. Strain through a fine sieve, discarding the solids.

5. Drizzle the verbena syrup over the cake, top with whipped cream if desired, garnish with the berries, and serve.

KENDRICK'S

5 CHESTNUT STREET

508-228-9156

WWW.THEQUAKERHOUSE.COM

SEASON: APRIL THROUGH DECEMBER

If you've ever wanted to see hospitality personified, come to Kendrick's at the Quaker House for dinner at eight o'clock on a Saturday night in July. At other busy restaurants, the hosts might be caught up in the throes of this frantic time of year. This is never the case at Kendrick's, where owner Stephanie Silva personally welcomes you into her restaurant. Stephanie is a dynamic woman in her early thirties—attractive, blond, and full of life. At the door, she will flash a genuine, happy-to-see-you smile because she is. When she's not at the door, Stephanie flies around the room, chatting at each table, assuring herself that every detail of her guests' experience is as perfect as she can make it. That means she spends her fair share of time refilling water glasses, busing tables, and running food.

Like many Nantucket restaurateurs, Stephanie has had a long history in the restaurant business, but unlike many, much

of it was right here on Nantucket, where her parents grew up and where she lived every summer until she moved here full-time when she was twenty-one. Stephanie began her career in restaurants at the age of twelve, when she went to work for her aunt, Jane Silva, at the Galley. In those days, the Galley had a little window in the kitchen that faced onto the beach, and Stephanie and her cousins would serve hot dogs, brownies, and their special "half-and-half" drinks (half lemonade, half iced tea) to bathing-suit-clad beachgoers. At seventeen, Stephanie got her first "real" restaurant job at Le Languedoc, where she worked on and off for twelve years. It was there that she learned the lesson she has since taken to heart at Kendrick's: be hospitable, at all times, no matter what.

Her very first job was at the tiny 'Sconset Café, where she worked for two seasons, first as the third chef—or the extra pair of hands under the chef and sous-chef—and then as the chef. Although the venue was small, Stephanie learned a lot, both from the chefs she worked under the first year, and from all her experimenting during the second. In between, she wintered in Vermont cooking at two little Italian restaurants.

But all the while she was living in Vermont, her mind kept wandering west. From all the books and food magazines she devoured, San Francisco seemed like the place to really hone her skills. After all, at the time, it was the epicenter of new American cuisine. It was where the wine country was, where Alice Waters was, and that's where Stephanie went as soon as she could, buying a car on Nantucket and driving it across country.

As soon as she got to San Francisco she began searching for work, but after dropping off her résumé all over town, she was anxious about being able to find a job, especially since her experience didn't look like much once she set it down on paper. She didn't even own her own set of knives! But everything came together when she walked into Zuni, Judy Rogers's famous restaurant. They had just lost someone that day and really needed a replacement. Stephanie became one of fourteen line cooks, beginning in the cold station and working her way up. It was a defining experience. Not only did she solidify and expand her culinary technique, she also began to develop a cooking style. At Zuni, everything was made from

scratch, from the stocks to curing the anchovies, and Stephanie saw firsthand the importance of perfect ingredients. She also saw more kinds of ingredients than she ever had seen before, especially produce. On her days off, she liked to peruse farmers' markets and admire row after row of gorgeous organic vegetables.

Now Stephanie has an intense reverence for ingredients, demanding that at Kendrick's, each one is treated as if it were going to be the only one on the plate. The result is simple, refined, perfectly cooked food without fancy garnishes to distract the diner.

After eight months in San Francisco, Stephanie found herself missing Nantucket. She had been spending a lot of time on the phone with her friend Rick Anderson, also a chef on Nantucket, and they decided that they would team up and open a restaurant together. Although he wanted to cook, they would create the menus together, and Stephanie would oversee the front of the house. It took them two years to find a space for Kendrick's, but true to their natures, they managed to keep busy. In the summers, they worked as private chefs, and in the winters, the searching continued, and Stephanie went back to Le Languedoc.

Finally, in 1996, they heard that the Quaker House Inn and Restaurant were going up for sale, and Stephanie knew that the historic building (built in 1847), with its big windows and wood plank floors, would be an ideal spot for their dream restaurant.

The two bought the building and, using all of the advantages of their youth, energy, and passion for making things beautiful, renovated the house themselves (Rick was a carpenter as well as a chef). They did everything from modernizing the tiny kitchen (which has the distinction of being Nantucket's smallest) to revamping the dining room, bar, and the eight cozy guest rooms upstairs.

Now, the two small dining rooms are elegantly appointed, with white cloth-covered tables and mismatched antique wooden chairs, flickering candles, and wildflowers on the tables and mantel. In the front room is a deep, comfortable bar where you often find regulars enjoying a leisurely meal by themselves, or having a glass of wine and appetizers with a friend. Next to the bar hangs an authentic whaling harpoon that serves as the restaurant's logo, reiterating the historic Nantucket feeling of the room.

After all this time, Stephanie finally has a place of her own. Although Rick no longer cooks (he went back full-time to his other love, carpentry), Stephanie decided to replace him rather than begin cooking herself, though she does admit to stepping in seamlessly whenever her chef is sick or the restaurant is "in the weeds"—very busy. Still, no matter what, she is always at the door when her customers arrive, smiling so graciously that regulars know her warm welcome isn't merely insurance against a barren February—it's simply an expression of who she is.

MENU

Lobster and Asparagus Soup

Kendrick's Famous Spring Rolls

Sesame-Crusted Salmon with Asian
Greens, Jasmine Rice, and Sweet Soy

Crème Brûlée

Lobster and Asparagus Soup

Have the fishmonger kill the lobsters and cut them into pieces for you—but only on the day you plan to cook them.

Serves 6 to 8

FOR THE LOBSTER STOCK

2 tablespoons olive oil

2 lobsters (about 1½ pounds each), claws separated, bodies halved and cleaned, tails split (see sidebar, page 129)

2 cups chopped carrots

1 cup chopped celery

1 cup chopped parsnips

1 cup chopped leeks

1 cup chopped onion

Salt and freshly ground black pepper, to taste

1 large tomato, roughly chopped

1 garlic clove, peeled and smashed

1 bay leaf

2½ quarts cold water

FOR THE SOUP

1 tablespoon olive oil

1 bunch of asparagus, trimmed, stalks roughly chopped, tips reserved for garnish

¼ cup chopped celery

¼ cup chopped parsnip

¼ cup chopped Vidalia onion

¼ cup chopped carrot

1 garlic clove

½ teaspoon salt, or to taste

Freshly ground black pepper, to taste

3 cups chicken broth

2 cups lobster stock

1 cup heavy cream

Lobster tail and claw meat, for garnish

1. To prepare the lobster stock, in a large, heavy stockpot, heat the oil over medium heat. Add the lobster bodies (reserving the tail and claws), carrots, celery, parsnips, leeks, onion, salt, and pepper, and cook, stirring occasionally, for 3 to 5 minutes, until the vegetables are wilted. Reduce the heat and cook for 10 minutes longer. Add the tomato, garlic, and bay leaf, and cook for 5 more minutes. Add the water, bring to a boil, and simmer for 20 minutes.

2. Drop the lobster claws and tail into the stock and cook for 3 to 5 minutes, or until the meat is opaque. Transfer the claws and tail to a plate and set aside to use for garnish. When cool enough to handle, cut the tail meat into 1-inch chunks. Remove the claw meat from the shells and reserve (see sidebar, page 77).

3. Strain the stock through a fine sieve into a large bowl. Reserve 2 cups of stock for the soup; keep the rest for another purpose (lobster stock will keep, frozen, for up to 6 months).

4. To prepare the soup, in a large saucepan, heat ½ tablespoon of the oil over high heat. Add the asparagus stalks, celery, parsnip, onion, carrot, garlic, salt, and pepper and cook, stirring, for 5 minutes. Add the chicken broth and bring to a boil. Lower the heat and simmer for 20 minutes. Add the lobster stock and cream, raise the heat, and bring to a boil. Simmer for 2 minutes. Turn off the heat and let the soup cool slightly.

5. Using a blender or food processor, purée the soup until smooth. Do this in batches if necessary.

6. In a large skillet, heat the remaining ½ tablespoon of oil over high heat. Add the lobster tail and claw meat and asparagus tips and sauté, stirring, for 3 minutes.

7. Gently reheat the soup just before serving. Ladle it into bowls. Divide the lobster meat and asparagus tips among them and serve at once.

To Prepare Lobsters for Stock

1. Insert a sharp knife into the head and pull forward to split the head.
2. While holding the lobster upside down, insert the knife where the tail meets the body, and split down the middle.
3. Remove the tomalley—the green substance—and rinse the innards.
4. Remove the tail meat and reserve for another use.
5. Remove the arms with claws attached and reserve for another use.
6. Use a hammer, meat cleaver, or the dull side of a knife to smash the lobster bodies.

Kendrick's Famous Spring Rolls

Makes 8 to 12 spring rolls;
serves 4 to 6

1 pound cleaned calamari

1 pound shrimp, shelled and deveined

1 cup very thinly sliced leeks

2 teaspoons sesame oil

1 tablespoon sambal oelek (fresh
  ground red chili paste)

½ bunch of Thai or regular basil,
  washed, dried, and julienned

1 large egg

1 cup water

12 sheets of spring roll pastry (see Note,
   page 131)

3 cups peanut oil, for frying

¾ cup cornstarch

1. To prepare the spring roll filling, in the bowl of a food processor purée the calamari and shrimp for 15 seconds, to a rough, chunky paste. Transfer to a bowl and stir in the leeks.

2. In a large saucepan over high heat, warm the sesame oil until it is almost smoking, then add the seafood-leek mixture. Add the sambal oelek (the mixture should turn light pink) and sauté over high heat until the ingredients are cooked through, approximately 5 minutes. Transfer the mixture to a strainer set above a bowl and let cool. Transfer to a bowl and stir in the basil.

3. To assemble the spring rolls, in a small bowl, combine the egg and ¼ cup of the water and beat lightly with a fork. Lay out a sheet of pastry with one corner facing toward you and place ¼ cup of filling along the center. Fold the side corners in toward each other, then bring the bottom corner up to meet them. Finally, roll up from the bottom toward the top corner, brushing with egg wash to seal. (Spring rolls can be formed, covered with plastic, and refrigerated for up to 4 hours before frying.)

4. To fry the rolls, in a large saucepan or wok, heat the peanut oil to 375°F. In a wide dish, combine the cornstarch and the remaining ¾ cup of water, and stir well. With a brush, coat the rolls in the cornstarch mixture, then drop them into the oil and fry for 2 to 3 minutes, until golden brown. Drain on a plate lined with a paper towel and serve immediately.

Note: Spring roll pastry is available at Asian specialty markets and is also carried by some large supermarkets.

Sesame-Crusted Salmon with Asian Greens, Jasmine Rice, and Sweet Soy

Serves 6

FOR THE SWEET SOY

1 cup sugar

½ cup water

1 cup fresh orange juice

½ cup soy sauce

Juice of 1 lemon, strained

Juice of 1 lime, strained

2 pods of star anise

1 tablespoon whole cumin seeds

1 tablespoon whole coriander seeds

One 1-inch piece of fresh ginger, peeled and roughly chopped

1 small jalapeño pepper, cut in half lengthwise, seeds removed

FOR THE JASMINE RICE

3 cups chicken broth or salted water

1½ cups jasmine rice

FOR THE SALMON

6 skinless salmon fillets (about 8 ounces each)

Salt and freshly ground black pepper, to taste

½ cup white sesame seeds

½ cup black sesame seeds

⅓ cup peanut oil

Pickled ginger and/or chopped scallion, for garnish

FOR THE GREENS

½ cup canola oil

¼ cup soy sauce

¼ cup rice wine vinegar

2 tablespoons sesame oil

¼ cup whole mint leaves plus 1 teaspoon chopped mint

2 tablespoons whole cilantro leaves plus 2 teaspoons chopped fresh cilantro

1 teaspoon freshly grated peeled ginger

1 teaspoon dried red pepper flakes

1 teaspoon mustard powder

5 cups mixed salad greens, such as baby
bok choy, tatsoi, mizuna, baby
spinach, and baby romaine lettuce,
washed and dried

1 small English cucumber, peeled,
seeded, and julienned

1. For the sweet soy, in a small saucepan over medium-high heat, bring the sugar and water to a boil, stirring to dissolve the sugar. When the sugar is dissolved, cook the mixture without stirring until golden brown and caramelized, about 7 minutes. Carefully pour in the orange juice (stand back; it may splatter and hiss) and bring the mixture back to a boil, whisking to combine. Add the soy sauce, lemon juice, lime juice, star anise, cumin seeds, coriander seeds, ginger, and jalapeño and whisk well. Reduce the heat to low and simmer for 10 to 15 minutes, or until the mixture thickens and foams. Remove from the heat, strain, and let cool. If the sauce is too thick to be drizzled, add a little water. Set aside.

2. To prepare the rice, in a small saucepan, bring the broth or salted water to a boil. Add the rice, reduce the heat to low, cover, and cook for about 20 minutes, or until tender. Remove from heat and set aside.

3. To prepare the fish, preheat the oven to 400°F. Season the fillets generously with salt and pepper, then sprinkle one side of the tops of the fillets with the white sesame seeds and the other side with the black. In an ovenproof sauté pan large enough to accommodate all of the fillets (or use two), heat the peanut oil just until it smokes. Sear the fillets for 1 minute, sesame side down. Flip the fillets and transfer the pan to the oven for about 5 minutes, or until just barely opaque in the center.

4. For the dressing, in a jar with a tight-fitting lid, add the oil, soy sauce, vinegar, sesame oil, chopped mint, chopped cilantro, ginger, red pepper flakes, and mustard powder; shake well and set aside.

5. In a medium bowl, add the salad greens, cucumber, whole mint leaves, and whole cilantro leaves. Toss to combine and set aside.

6. Arrange a scoop of the jasmine rice in the bottom of 6 shallow bowls. Reshake the dressing and pour it over the salad greens. Gently toss. Divide the greens among the bowls on top of the rice. Place a salmon fillet on the greens, and drizzle with a healthy stream of sweet soy. Garnish with the pickled ginger and/or chopped scallion and serve.

Crème Brûlée

Serves 6

2 cups heavy cream

4 large egg yolks

⅓ cup granulated sugar

½ vanilla bean, halved lengthwise and scraped

3 tablespoons superfine sugar

1. Preheat the oven to 350°F. To prepare the custard, in a medium bowl, whisk together the cream, egg yolks, granulated sugar, and vanilla scrapings. Strain the mixture through a fine sieve, then divide it among six 4-ounce ramekins.

2. Arrange the ramekins in a baking pan and place it on the oven rack. Pour enough very hot water into the baking pan to reach two thirds of the way up the sides of the ramekins. Cover the baking pan with foil and prick in a few places with a knife. Bake the custards for 40 to 45 minutes, or until set around the edges but still slightly loose in the center. Transfer the ramekins to a rack and let cool, then cover and refrigerate for at least 6 hours or overnight.

3. Right before serving, sprinkle a thin, even coating of the superfine sugar on the surface of each custard. Use a preheated broiler or a blowtorch to caramelize the sugar. It will take about 1 to 2 minutes in a broiler, about 30 seconds with a blowtorch.

LE LANGUEDOC

24 BROAD STREET

508-228-2552

WWW.LELANGUEDOC.COM

SEASON: MAY THROUGH MID-DECEMBER

How often do you walk into a restaurant where you are warmly greeted by name, presented with not one, but two outstanding menus, then graciously escorted to your choice of one of three unique dining venues?

It's certainly rare, and can't be easy, but under the seasoned, professional direction of master chef Neil Grennan and master of the house Alan M. Cunha, Le Languedoc provides diners with just that. Multiply two floors by six dining rooms by two menus and you get a seemingly unending number of choices. And when everything on both menus is sure to be top-notch, you'll be happy going bistro or haute, mixing foie gras with the best burger on the island.

The restaurant was named by the original owners, the Martys, after their native region in southern France. Its decor and menus have retained their unique blend of French influence and old-fashioned New England sensibility since 1975, when Le Languedoc was handed over to Alan, Neil, and brother Eddie Grennan, all of whom were in their twenties. Alan took charge of the front of the house, Eddie took on management of the guest rooms above the restaurant and in the guest house down the block, and Neil began to work his magic in the kitchen.

Along with Michael Shannon of the Club Car and Jean-Charles Berruet of the Chanticleer, Neil Grennan completes the triumvirate of master chefs on Nantucket. He developed his love of cooking as a child growing up in Concord, Massachusetts, where his grandmother was an expert cook and baker. Neil fell into the restaurant business at the early age of twelve, when his older brothers roped him into washing dishes on a particularly busy Mother's Day at a nearby Howard Johnson's. He immediately got caught up in the whole excitement of a restaurant kitchen, and he continued working in restaurants in all different capacities through high school and college.

Neil experienced his first really creative cooking job when he was hired as the innkeeper at Dana Place in Jackson, New Hampshire. He covered for the chef, Hugh Dakers, on his day off. Hugh became a hugely formative influence on Neil, who watched the way the chef would write his ever-changing menus each day, created in combination from what was in season and what he had on hand.

Several years later, Neil joined forces with his brother Eddie, and together they opened their first restaurant, the General Warren Tavern in Charlestown, just outside of Boston. They were anxious at first, since neither one of them had that many years of experience. But they were excited and eager and the Tavern took off, becoming a destination restaurant for local politicians, journalists, and affluent business people. Alan was at a local college when he was hired on as a bartender, and he eventually rose through the ranks to general manager. Although business was good, the Grennans decided to form a partnership with Alan and sell the restaurant in order to open something new. They gave themselves a year to look, and they searched all over New England for an appropriate spot. It was Eddie who lured them to Nantucket, where he had a house. There, they heard about an older, hard-working French couple who were ready to sell their beloved business. Al-

though naysayers warned them against it (the price seemed high at the time), the partners went ahead and purchased Le Languedoc. And they've never regretted it since.

In the years that followed, Neil continued to develop his culinary skills, adding his signature style to the restaurant's French menu. He keeps up with culinary trends by reading voraciously and traveling to eat in the best New York and Boston restaurants. In 1990, Neil hired Mark Yelle to be the chef de cuisine, though Neil still oversees the operation as the executive chef–owner and keeps the kitchen organized and flowing.

While Neil is making sure everything is running smoothly in the kitchen, Alan, the self-described ringmaster of this three-ring circus, manages the front of the house with panache. He is in constant motion, polishing a crystal wine glass here, welcoming a guest by name there, heartily laughing at someone's joke somewhere else. He manages the whole affair with such skill that you know he really means it when he says the table will be yours in twenty minutes. Even if you're a first-time guest, you can expect the friendliest of welcomes and the most attentive service. Whether you choose to dine upstairs or down, inside or out, rest assured you're in for a treat.

If you elect to sit downstairs, you'll discover a zinc-topped wooden bar with seven barstools and a casual bistro-style dining room often filled to the brim with the many

regulars who dine at Le Languedoc. It's hard not to feel at home in this intimate, low-ceilinged room. On a balmy summer eve, you might request a table on the restaurant's canopy-covered patio—a favorite spot of many guests. Whether you're inside, seated in the café, or outside on the patio, you can order dishes from either the café or dining-room menu, mixing and matching as desired. So if you're craving the savory sweetbreads from the dining room for an appetizer and a tempting risotto from the bistro menu for your main course, don't worry—you can have both.

If you're in the mood for a more formal dining experience, you can make a reservation upstairs for one of the decorous dining rooms, where you'll be content sticking to the more refined dining-room menu. The front two rooms are painted a warm,

sunny yellow, with large windows that look out onto Broad Street. Antique Windsor chairs, original artwork, and handsome oak hutches create an elegant yet comfortable setting where you can enjoy your repast in style. There is also a charming private dining room furnished with a single antique mahogany dining table that could easily be found in any grand Nantucket home.

Once you've decided where to dine, you're faced with an even more challenging task: what to order. Each year, the menu is revised and updated to keep up with current trends, but there are several items that Neil wouldn't dream of removing—his devoted following would surely declare mutiny! Neil's Caesar salad is hands-down the island's best, his Black Angus tenderloin with parisienne potatoes, peppercorn demi-glace, and sauce béarnaise is another favorite. The delicate lobster bisque is simply a Nantucket classic.

As for beverages, Neil and Alan have kept the wine list at an approachable size. Rather than stocking thousands of bottles, they've expertly chosen a manageable selection of affordable French and Californian wines, as well as an assortment of special-occasion wines and spirits.

Exquisite cooking and gracious hosting have given Neil and Alan the enviable gift of a loyal regular clientele. In fact, according to Alan, repeat customers make up about 65 percent of the restaurant's business. And the pleasure that Neil and Alan take in what they do is apparent in the way they manage their restaurant. They are both perfectionists and pay meticulous attention to detail in all aspects of their business. The consummate restaurateur-host Alan expresses his philosophy this way: "Ours is a business of positive energy and a business of detail.

Everyone that comes to our door is given the recognition and respect he or she deserves. We try to achieve consistency in all aspects: in our food, our wine, and our service."

This kind of professionalism and respect doesn't stop with the customers. Neil and Alan have great consideration for their staff, who are just as loyal, returning year after year and becoming part of the Languedoc family. Some of them even are family, like Mark's wife, Eithne, who waits tables. In their minds, Neil and Alan believe that people don't work *for* you, but *with* you. It's important for them to give back to the community by hiring people who live on the island, which inspires trust and a greater sense of ownership.

And they must be doing something right. How else can you explain why Le Languedoc has remained one of the most loved restaurants on Nantucket for the past quarter century?

MENU

Le Languedoc Lobster Bisque

Escargot and Sweetbread Ragout in a
Pastry Cup with Pommes Anna Top Hat

Roasted Monkfish with Garlic Clam Broth
and Broccoli Rabe

LuLu's Flourless Chocolate Torte

Le Languedoc
Lobster Bisque

Serves 6 to 8

5 tablespoons butter

1 small onion, chopped

½ cup diced carrot

One 1½-pound uncooked lobster, freshly
   killed (see Note, page 144)

2 tablespoons curry powder

1 tablespoon tomato paste

2 sprigs of fresh flat-leaf parsley,
   chopped

1 bay leaf

Pinch of fresh thyme leaves

3 tablespoons cognac

½ cup dry white wine

½ cup chicken broth or lobster stock

1 tablespoon Madeira

4 cups heavy cream

¼ cup flour

Salt and freshly ground black pepper,
   to taste

Chopped fresh chives, for garnish

1. In a heavy stockpot over medium heat, melt 2 tablespoons of the butter and sauté the onion and carrot until transparent, about 10 minutes.

2. Crack the lobster and remove the meat, reserving the shells. Add the lobster meat, curry powder, tomato paste, and herbs to the pot and sauté for another 5 minutes.

3. Pour in the cognac and carefully ignite, using a match or a small kitchen blowtorch to start the flame, then allow the alcohol to burn off.

4. Add the wine and broth or stock and simmer for 20 minutes. Remove the pieces of lobster meat and allow to cool. Dice the meat and mix it with the Madeira in a small bowl. Set aside.

5. Reduce the heat to medium-low. Crack the lobster shells into smaller pieces, add them to the stock, and let simmer for 1 hour.

6. In a small saucepan over medium heat, melt the remaining 3 tablespoons of butter. Meanwhile, in another saucepan over medium heat, bring the cream to a slight boil.

7. When the butter has melted, sprinkle in the flour and blend thoroughly with a whisk.

Once the cream reaches a boil, add it slowly to the butter and flour mixture, whisking until smooth.

8. To finish the bisque, transfer the stock to a fine sieve set over a large, heatproof bowl and strain, discarding the solids. Rinse out the stockpot and pour the strained stock back into the pot. Whisk in the cream mixture and stir in the Madeira-soaked lobster meat. Season to taste, ladle into soup bowls, and sprinkle with the chopped chives.

Note: See the sidebar on page 129 or have your fishmonger do the dirty work and kill the lobster for you—but only on the day you plan to prepare this recipe.

Escargot and Sweetbread Ragout in a Pastry Cup with Pommes Anna Top Hat

If you love sweetbreads but don't have the time or inclination to make the whole recipe (meaning the pastry cup, top hat, etc.), the ragout is delicious on its own.

Serves 6

FOR THE SWEETBREADS

- 2 cups water
- 1 cup white wine
- 1 carrot, peeled and chopped
- 1 onion, chopped
- 1 celery stalk, chopped
- ½ lemon
- 1 tablespoon pickling spice
- 1 pound sweetbreads

FOR THE PASTRY

- 1 cup water
- 8 tablespoons (1 stick) unsalted butter
- 1 cup all-purpose flour, sifted
- 4 large eggs
- 1 tablespoon finely grated Parmesan cheese
- Pinch of salt and freshly ground black pepper

FOR THE POTATOES

- 6 to 8 tablespoons peanut oil
- 4 large Yukon Gold potatoes (about 1½ pounds), peeled and sliced ⅛ inch thick
- Salt and freshly ground black pepper, to taste

CONTINUED

⅓ pound salsify (about 2 large stalks),
  peeled and cut into ½-inch dice

20 asparagus spears, trimmed into 2-inch
  tips

3 cups water, plus additional for the
  beets

1 cup fresh, shelled cranberry beans

2 sprigs of fresh thyme

2 bay leaves

½ cup cider vinegar

½ cup sugar

1 tablespoon pickling spice

1 pound small golden beets, scrubbed
  and trimmed

2 tablespoons peanut oil

¾ cup all-purpose flour

2 tablespoons minced shallots

2 tablespoons minced garlic

1 cup demi-glace or rich beef broth

¼ cup Madeira

2 tablespoons brandy

20 cooked snails (shucked if fresh)

1 tablespoon chopped fresh thyme
  Salt and freshly ground black pepper,
  to taste

1 tablespoon unsalted butter

2 large red bell peppers, roasted, peeled,
  and cut into ¼-inch strips (see
  sidebar, page 148)

1. Prepare the sweetbreads the day before or early in the morning. In a large pot, bring the water, wine, carrot, onion, celery, lemon, and pickling spice to a boil, lower the heat, and simmer for 20 minutes. Add the sweetbreads and poach until firm and cooked through, about 10 to 15 minutes. Fill a bowl with ice water. Transfer the poached sweetbreads to the ice water, let cool, then drain and pat dry.

2. Clean the sweetbreads by removing any membranes and fat. Lay the sweetbreads out on a baking sheet lined with parchment paper. Cover with another sheet of parchment and place another baking pan on top, weighted down with a 1- to 2-pound can or jar. Refrigerate for 8 hours or overnight. Break the sweetbreads up into bite-size pieces.

3. To prepare the pastry, preheat the oven to 350°F. Line a baking sheet with parchment paper and spray with a nonstick cooking spray. In a saucepan over high heat, bring the water and butter to a boil. When the butter is melted, add the flour all at once, stirring, and beat to form a ball. Turn off the heat and add the eggs one at a time, stirring well in between each addition. Stir in the cheese, salt, and pepper.

4. Place the dough in a pastry bag with a large plain tip. Pipe the dough into mounds 2 to 3 inches in diameter and 2 to 3 inches high, spacing them at least 2 inches apart

on the baking sheet. (Alternately, spoon the dough into the mounds.) Bake the pastries for about 35 minutes, until puffed up and browned. Do not disturb them as they bake. Transfer to a wire rack to cool. Cut the tops off the puffs and scoop out the doughy centers. Reserve the puffs, discarding the centers.

5. To prepare the potatoes, in a small nonstick pan, heat 1 tablespoon of the oil over high heat. Arrange 8 to 10 of the potato slices in an overlapping circle in the pan and season with salt and pepper. Cook slowly, swirling around in the pan a bit so that they brown and don't stick, until tender and browned on one side, about 10 minutes. Set aside on a baking sheet and continue with the remaining potato slices and oil. Reheat the potatoes in a 300°F. oven before serving.

6. To prepare the ragout, fill a bowl with ice water. Bring a pot of salted water to a boil. Add the salsify and cook for 5 minutes. Transfer the blanched salsify to the ice water to cool; use a slotted spoon to remove the salsify, shake off any excess water, and set aside. Return the water to a boil and add the asparagus tips. Cook for 3 minutes (until bright green and tender), then transfer immediately to the ice water, adding more ice if necessary. Drain and set aside.

7. Place 3 cups of the water in a small saucepan and add the cranberry beans, sprigs of thyme, and bay leaves. Bring to a boil over high heat, then lower the heat to medium-low and simmer for 15 to 20 minutes, or until the beans are tender but not mushy. Drain, remove the bay leaves, and set aside.

8. In a medium saucepan over medium-high heat, combine the vinegar, sugar, and pickling spice and bring to a simmer. Add the beets and enough water to cover. Bring the mixture to a boil and cook until the beets are tender, about 30 to 45 minutes. Drain and let cool. When cool enough to handle, peel the beets, cut them into cubes, and set aside.

9. In a sauté pan, heat the peanut oil over high heat. Dredge the prepared sweetbreads in the flour and sauté until brown, 3 to 4 minutes per side. Transfer to a platter lined with a paper towel and set aside.

10. Turn down the heat to low under the sauté pan, add the shallots and garlic, and cook for 1 minute. Add the demi-glace, Madeira, and brandy and cook the mixture, scraping up any browned bits stuck to the bottom of the pan, until the mixture is reduced to a glaze, about 6 minutes. Add the snails, chopped thyme, sweetbreads, and cranberry beans and simmer for 1 to 2 minutes to heat through. Taste and season with salt and pepper.

11. In a saucepan over medium heat, melt the butter. Add the salsify, asparagus, and roasted peppers and heat, covered, until warmed through, about 2 minutes.

LE LANGUEDOC

12. To serve, place the ragout in the center of the puffs. Place the puffs on plates and top each one with a warm potato cake (place the cake on an angle). Spoon the vegetables around the puffs and serve immediately.

Roasting Bell Peppers

Place the pepper directly on a gas burner over medium heat and blacken on all sides, turning occasionally with tongs, about 10 minutes. Put the pepper in a bowl and cover with a plate. Set aside for 10 to 15 minutes, or until the skin easily peels away. Place the pepper on a cutting board and gently scrape away the blackened skin with the back of a knife. Cut the pepper open, remove the seeds, stems, and any thick membranes, and slice as directed.

Roasted Monkfish
with Garlic Clam Broth
and Broccoli Rabe

Chef Mark Yelle likes the way the sweetness of the fish, smokiness of the pancetta, bitterness of the broccoli rabe, and brininess of the clams play off one another in this inventive dish.

Serves 4

1 pound broccoli rabe, trimmed	20 littleneck clams, scrubbed
1 carrot, peeled and julienned or thinly sliced	1 tablespoon chopped fresh thyme
1 small ripe tomato	1 tablespoon chopped scallions
½ pound pancetta, diced	1 tablespoon fresh lemon juice, strained
7 tablespoons unsalted butter	½ teaspoon cracked pink peppercorns
2 tablespoons minced shallots	Salt and freshly ground black pepper, to taste
2 tablespoons minced garlic	3 tablespoons olive oil
2 cups white wine	Four 6-ounce portions of monkfish
2 cups water	

1. Fill a large bowl with ice water. Bring 2 quarts of salted water to a boil. Add the broccoli rabe and cook for 4 minutes, then transfer to the ice water to cool. Use a slotted spoon to remove the broccoli rabe and shake off any excess water; set aside. Return the water to a boil. Add the carrot and cook for 1 minute. Transfer to the ice water to cool, adding more ice if necessary. Use a slotted spoon to remove the carrot and shake off any excess water; set aside. Bring the water back to a boil. Add the tomato and blanch for 30 seconds, then use a slotted spoon to transfer to the ice water to cool. When cool enough to handle, core and peel the tomato with a paring knife, then halve, seed, and cut into small cubes. Set aside.

2. In a medium skillet, cook the pancetta until crisp, about 5 minutes. Drain on paper towels.

3. In a deep sauté pan over medium heat, melt 3 tablespoons of the butter. Add the shallots and garlic and cook, stirring, until softened, about 2 minutes. Raise the heat, add the wine and water, cover, and bring to a boil. Add the clams and cook for 3 to 5 minutes. Using a slotted spoon, transfer the clams as they open to a bowl and set aside, covering to keep warm.

4. When all the clams are out of the broth, add the pancetta, tomato cubes, and thyme and let the broth reduce by half, 10 to 15 minutes. Turn off the heat and stir in 2 tablespoons of the butter, the scallions, lemon juice, pink peppercorns, and salt and pepper. If the broth is too intense, stir in a little water to cut it.

5. Preheat the oven to 350°F. To prepare the fish, in a large, ovenproof sauté pan, heat the oil over medium-high heat. Season the fish with salt and pepper, add to the pan, and cook for 30 seconds. Flip the fish, add the remaining 2 tablespoons of butter, and cook for 30 seconds more. Place the pan in the oven for 8 minutes, or until the flesh turns opaque.

6. Just before serving, reheat the broccoli rabe in a hot sauté pan with just a splash of water and salt and pepper to taste.

7. Make beds of broccoli rabe and carrot in 4 soup plates and top with the fish. Spoon over the broth, garnish with clams, and serve.

Chef de cuisine Mark Yelle.

LuLu's Flourless Chocolate Torte

Laurie "LuLu" Donovan worked at Le Languedoc for seven years, both on the line and in the trenches as the restaurant's pastry chef. We're proud to include her recipe for this sinfully rich chocolate torte.

Serves 6 to 8

FOR THE TORTE

⅓ cup cocoa, sifted, plus additional for dusting the pan

9 ounces bittersweet chocolate, chopped

1 cup (2 sticks) unsalted butter

¾ cup sugar

⅓ cup heavy cream

1 teaspoon vanilla extract

5 large eggs

Raspberries, blackberries, and fresh mint sprigs, for garnish

FOR THE CRÈME ANGLAISE

2 cups milk

¼ cup sugar

1 vanilla bean, split lengthwise

4 large egg yolks

1. Preheat the oven to 350°F. Grease the bottom of a 9-inch cake pan and line with parchment or waxed paper; grease the parchment. Dust the greased pan with cocoa, tapping out any excess.

2. To prepare the torte, in the top of a double boiler over simmering water, melt the chocolate and ½ cup of the butter. Turn off the heat and let cool. In a separate saucepan over medium-low heat, combine the remaining ½ cup of butter with the sugar, cream, and vanilla. Stir the mixture until the sugar dissolves. In a large bowl, whisk together the eggs and the ⅓ cup of cocoa. Slowly whisk in the cream mixture. Add the melted chocolate mixture and whisk until incorporated.

3. Pour the batter into the prepared cake pan and bake for 25 to 35 minutes, or until the center of the torte is just set. Transfer to a wire rack and let cool slightly.

4. Meanwhile, prepare the crème anglaise. In a saucepan over medium heat, combine the

milk, sugar, and vanilla bean and bring to a simmer, stirring occasionally. In a small bowl, whisk the egg yolks. Add a small amount of the hot cream mixture to the yolks, whisking constantly. Slowly whisk in the remaining cream mixture. Return the mixture to the saucepan and cook, stirring, over low heat until the custard thickens enough to coat the back of a wooden spoon. Pour the custard through a fine sieve into a bowl and let cool.

5. While the cake is still slightly warm, cut out 6 to 8 rounds with a 2 1/2- to 3-inch cookie cutter or metal ring. (Or simply slice the torte into 6 to 8 wedges.) Pour a small pool of crème anglaise onto the center of each dessert plate and top with a round of torte. Garnish with fresh raspberries, blackberries, and sprigs of mint.

ÒRAN MÓR

2 SOUTH BEACH STREET

508-228-8655

WWW.NANTUCKET.NET/FOOD/ORANMOR

SEASON: YEAR-ROUND

Òran Mór is a Gaelic phrase meaning "great song"; in Scottish tradition, every clan has its own great song. Kathleen and Peter Wallace chose this melodic name for their restaurant to sing of their love for their family, Peter's respect for his Scottish heritage, and their pride in creating a truly harmonious and distinctive venue. It is also a name with a lilting sound and an eye-catching unusualness to it, one that the Wallaces feel captures a certain Nantucket mood—the evanescent romance of the island's moors on a foggy spring evening.

As a restaurant, Òran Mór encapsulates the romance of the Wallaces as well. It is a very personal reflection of who they are—individually, as a couple, and as a family. Before its present incarnation, the upstairs at 2 South Beach Street, located in an old house above an antiques shop, was another appropriately named restaurant, Second Story. Almost twenty years ago, Kathleen and Peter had their first date there, and today they are as passionate about the space and about each other as they ever were. In Òran Mór, they have managed to build the very restaurant that they would love to go to themselves, a convivial spot with impeccable food served in a serene and lovely setting.

While Peter directs the kitchen and sends his skillful, minimalist creations to the dining room, Kathleen runs things up front. Her hand is apparent in the calm warm tones of the dining rooms, the friendly and flexible attitude of the wait staff, the awe-inspiring wine list, and the almost poetic style of the menu. In both kitchen and dining rooms, a great love for what they do shows in the minute ways they constantly try to improve upon their efforts.

Nantucket is very much a part of who the Wallaces are. Peter was practically born sailing, and as a child, when he and his family took vacations sailing around their hometown of Hingham (south of Boston), Nantucket was a favorite stop. Kathleen came to Nantucket later, after college. One of her first jobs on the island was as a sous-chef at the India House. That's where she met Peter, after he took over her job when she began working up front.

Peter didn't grow up planning to be a chef, but through working in restaurants during and after college, he picked up the food-loving bug. He attended the Culinary Institute of America and then worked in different parts of the country perfecting his skills. After cooking for a winter on St. Martin in the Caribbean, he found himself in need of a summertime gig and thought of Nantucket. There, he knew he could sail and build boats in the morning, and cook at night. Interestingly, Òran Mór is the second upstairs venture for the Wallaces. Their first restaurant was upstairs in a building in Manchester, Vermont, owned by Kathleen's mom. They opened as Up for Breakfast in 1986 and gained immediate cult status. At the time, Kathleen and Peter were taking turns cooking and caring for their one-year-old son, Dylan. During the fourteen months that they ran Up for Breakfast they also built a house and had another son, Connor. Peter would cook all morning, build the house until it got dark, then go back to do the preparation for the next morning and close up the restaurant for the day. Two days a week he would stay home

with the boys to give Kathleen a break—and her "break" included getting up at four A.M. to do the restaurant's breakfast!

In 1988, the Wallaces heard that the recently renovated Wauwinet Inn in Nantucket had built a world-class restaurant. Although Up for Breakfast was doing well, Peter and Kathleen both missed the ocean and their Nantucket life, and they figured this was the right opportunity to move back. In fact, Peter wanted the job so badly that instead of faxing his résumé as requested, he showed up on island and "forced himself" on the management team. Since executive chef Keith Mahoney had already been hired, Peter was hired on as sous-chef, and he and Kathleen sold Up for Breakfast and made the move. Peter worked at Topper's for a total of nine years—three as Keith's sous-chef, and six as the executive chef. During those years, Topper's grew into the nationally acclaimed destination restaurant that it still is today.

However, after nine years, Peter and Kathleen knew it was time to strike out on their own. They looked around for a place to open a restaurant, but they didn't find any that spoke to them until Second Story came up for lease. Their nostalgic spot had fallen into disrepair, and its location—somewhat removed from the beaten path—would have daunted prospective buyers without the experience, the confidence, and the affection for the room that Kathleen and Peter had. Kathleen had had experience renovating houses on the island for years, and in enthusiastic Nantucket style, she and Peter bought and completely renovated the space themselves—with some help from family and friends.

From the picturesque glimpse of the harbor that you get at the bar to the paint-spattered wooden floors, their creation is a fusing of the elegant and the rustic. The restaurant has three dining rooms, all painted creamy white with a soft celadon trim. The furnishings, many of which were built by Peter himself, are spare and taste-ful, with an almost Shaker aesthetic. One piece he is particularly proud of is the ter-rific half dory (small rowboat) that stands on end to serve as a wine rack for half bot-tles. Fittingly, all of the artwork is local, pre-dominantly featuring landscape paintings by Michael Moore.

Even the bar itself is a local artifact, having started out as the portico of the Pa-cific National Bank's original building on Washington Street. Kathleen and Peter res-cued it from the yard of a friend who had bought the building and intended to dump the imposing semicircle of carved wood. They dragged it back to the restaurant and completely overhauled it, using stretched, urethaned canvas for the top and adding a boat "rub rail" to the edge. It isn't unusual for diners to enjoy a full meal seated at this re-vamped piece of Nantucket history.

Kathleen's refined appreciation for de-tails gives a depth and sincerity to the Òran Mór experience. She insists that nothing in-terfere with the dining experience, and en-

sures that neither the music nor the other diners are distractingly loud. As jazz buffs, the Wallaces play only favorite recordings from their own classic jazz collection in the restaurant. The couple takes these details to heart, and they make sure that their staff does as well. In fact, working at Òran Mór is considered such a "great gig" that small-business owners can often be spotted moonlighting as wait staff in the off-season.

Along with Kathleen's sensibility, at the core of their success is Peter's cuisine, which perfectly embodies the integrity and pas-sion that drives Òran Mór. His philosophy is that simple presentation and few ingredi-ents are the perfect showcase for culinary accomplishment. By leaving some white space on the plate, Peter allows himself room to feature his perfected technique and avert the danger of confusing his guests with overly complicated layers of flavor. Peter calls his kitchen "a temple to ingredi-ents." He attributes the consistent superb quality of his ingredients to his loyalty to the island's farms and merchants.

Peter's menu features the pick of sea-sonal delicacies. Fresh fava beans are mashed atop toasts to accompany roast lamb in the spring. Perfect island tomatoes are served in simple glory, lightly marinated to make a salad imbued with the essence of summer. Peter is able to get sushi-grade fish, and he offers a sashimi of the day. Every dish is proof of Peter's talent and expertise. His knowledge of the island's fish and seafood is particularly extensive, not surprisingly, since he scallops and fishes commercially during the off-season.

Kathleen and Peter stress that the fabulous food and smooth-running service at Òran Mór are made possible with the invaluable help of Sidney and Jim Trond, the floor manager and sous-chef. The couple has worked with the Wallaces for over a decade. It adds to the family feel of the restaurant to see the wives up front, husbands in the kitchen, and the Wallaces' high-school-age sons working as busboys. As the boys grow up, working in the restaurant becomes an increasingly integral way for the family to spend time together.

As Peter says, with satisfaction, "It's exactly what I had in mind. When we have a Saturday night when both boys are on the floor and Kathleen is on the front and we have a great night, it's exactly the life that I want, and I'm just grateful we were able to pull it off."

MENU

Nantucket Oysters with Osetra Caviar

■

Grilled Shrimp in the
Style of Southern France

■

Grilled Whole Black Bass
with Fines-Herbes Pistou

■

Individual Strawberry-Rhubarb
Tarte Tatins

Nantucket Oysters with Osetra Caviar

This is chef Peter Wallace's favorite indulgent but no-fuss way to begin any Nantucket feast. The amount of caviar can be varied to suit your taste and budget. On Nantucket, we use our own local oysters from a farm off Polpis Harbor. Try to use oysters local to where you are. Rockweed is used to pack lobsters and can be obtained from your local fishmonger.

3 cold-water oysters per person, scrubbed

1 bunch of rockweed, for garnish
  Osetra caviar, as desired (1-ounce can serve 6, but more is nice, too)

1 lemon wedge per person
  Champagne, to sip

1. Open the oysters at the last minute before serving. Discard the top shell. (Or have your fishmonger do this for you.)

2. Make a bed of rockweed on each plate. Place three oyster shells on each plate and top each one with an oyster and a dollop of caviar. Garnish with a lemon wedge. Serve with plenty of ice-cold champagne.

ÒRAN MÓR

Grilled Shrimp in the Style of Southern France

Serves 6

3 plum tomatoes

2 tablespoons olive oil

3 garlic cloves, chopped

3 tablespoons chopped fresh flat-leaf
   parsley

½ cup white wine

18 large shrimp (1½ pounds total of
   "colossals"; 12 to a pound), shelled
   and deveined

Salt and freshly ground black pepper,
to taste

3 tablespoons drained capers

6 tablespoons (¾ stick) unsalted butter,
   cut into chunks

1. Bring a pot of water to a boil over high heat. Fill a bowl with ice water. Blanch the tomatoes in the boiling water for 1 minute. Drain and immediately transfer to the ice water. When cool enough to handle, slip off the skins, quarter the tomatoes, scrape out the seeds, and dice the flesh into ¼-inch cubes.

2. In a large sauté pan, heat the oil over high heat. Add the garlic and sauté for 1 minute. Add the diced tomatoes, parsley, and white wine. Let the sauce simmer, stirring occasionally, until almost all the liquid has evaporated, about 5 minutes.

3. Meanwhile, preheat and oil a grill or grill pan. Season the shrimp with salt and pepper and cook for 1 minute per side, until they just turn pink. Reserve the shrimp.

4. Add the capers to the sauce, reduce the heat, and slowly whisk in the butter, piece by piece. Toss the shrimp in the sauce, then arrange 3 shrimp on each plate. Cover with a spoonful of sauce and serve immediately.

Grilled Whole Black Bass with Fines-Herbes Pistou

Though Nantucket is famous for its striped bass, these must be over thirty-six inches long to be caught legally, and they have a very short season. The smaller black bass called for here are more widely available and have a sweet, tender flesh that lends itself well to this gorgeous, surprisingly simple recipe.

Serves 6

6 whole black bass (1½ to 2 pounds each), head on, gutted and scaled
 Extra-virgin olive oil to drizzle
 Salt and freshly ground black pepper, to taste
Two 16-ounce cans whole peeled tomatoes, or 2 pounds ripe fresh tomatoes, cored
2 bunches of fresh flat-leaf parsley, chopped

3 bunches of fresh chives, chopped
2 bunches of fresh lemon thyme, chopped
2 bunches of fresh basil, chopped
2 heads of garlic, peeled and slivered
6 lemons, thinly sliced into rounds, ends discarded

1. Preheat a grill to very hot. Preheat the oven to 350°F. Allow the fish to come to room temperature. Cut through the skin and into the flesh with the tip of a very sharp knife in a crosshatch pattern on both sides of each fish. Drizzle with olive oil and sprinkle with salt and pepper. Grill the fish for 5 minutes on each side.
2. Place the grilled fish side by side, head to tail, in a large roasting pan.
3. Place the tomatoes in a bowl and crush with your hands. Cover the fish with the crushed tomatoes. Mix together the chopped fresh herbs and sprinkle over the fish. Distribute the garlic over the fish. Lay the lemon slices in overlapping rows over each fish, like scales. Drizzle a little olive oil on top and roast for 20 to 30 minutes, or until the fish is opaque.
4. Serve each fish on a plate surrounded by tomatoes from the pan and drizzled with its own juices.

ÒRAN MÓR

Note: To gut and scale a round fish such as black bass, first remove its fins with a strong pair of scissors. Scale it by running a fish scaler or knife along the fish's skin from tail to head. Next, use the scissors to make a shallow cut along the underbody from just past the tail to just before the head. Cut and pull away the gills and the internal organs, and discard. Scrape the inside cavity of the fish, particularly along the vertebrae, to expose any blood, then rinse the inside of the fish thoroughly under cold water.

Individual Strawberry-Rhubarb Tarte Tatins

These elegant upside-down tarts can be made completely in advance.

Serves 6

1 pound puff pastry, thawed if frozen

3 cups sugar

1 cup water

6 cups rhubarb (about 12 stalks), peeled and cut into ½-inch pieces

1 pint medium strawberries, quartered

Grated zest from 1½ lemons

Whipped cream, for garnish

Mint sprigs, for garnish

1. Preheat the oven to 375°F. Roll the puff pastry out ¼ inch thick. Cut it into six 4½-inch rounds. Refrigerate the rounds (between sheets of waxed paper if necessary) until ready to use.

2. In a large, heavy-bottomed skillet, combine the sugar and water over medium heat, stirring until the sugar dissolves. Cook the mixture until deep golden brown and caramelized, swirling the pan to make sure the caramelization is even. It will take about 10 minutes.

3. Line a baking pan with parchment or waxed paper. In a bowl, combine the rhubarb, strawberries, and zest. Pile the mixture as high as possible into six 8-ounce ramekins and arrange them on the baking sheet. Ladle about ⅓ cup of caramel over the fruit in each ramekin and top with a round of puff pastry. Press down lightly.

4. Bake for 25 minutes, or until the top pastry is puffed and golden brown. Immediately remove the ramekins from the baking pan (the sugar will have oozed over the ramekins and will begin to harden, making them impossible to remove later!). Set the ramekins aside to cool to room temperature. Just before serving, turn the ramekins upside down onto plates so that the fruit filling tops the pastry. Garnish with whipped cream and mint.

ÒRAN MÓR

SHIP'S
INN

13 FAIR STREET

508-228-0040

WWW.NANTUCKET.NET/LODGING/SHIPSINN/RESTAURANT

SEASON: END OF MAY THROUGH FIRST WEEK OF DECEMBER

Mark Gottwald is one of Nantucket's most enviable restaurateurs, for not only does he run a popular and comfortably elegant restaurant, but he manages to fish to his heart's content, spend tons of quality time with his family, and produce movies to boot. Here is a man who knows how to cook, and how to live.

If you're up early enough, you might see Mark going out on the Nantucket waters in his commercial fishing boat to catch the fish he'll prepare that night at Ship's Inn, along with the highly prized tuna and striped bass that he sells to Japanese and American markets.

Mark is not just the owner of Ship's Inn, he is the person who styled the restaurant into what it is now, and it is his fervor for freshness and his fine-tuned knowledge of food that makes Ship's Inn an absolute must for any visitor to the island. The simplicity of Mark's approach allows

his inspired flavor combinations to shine through.

For example, you might start with a chilled soup of smoked tomato with lobster and avocado, in which the acidity of the tomatoes is tempered by dusky smoke, while the rich smoothness of lobster and avocado suddenly makes them the most natural partners in the world. Or try the seafood chowder, a Nantucket staple that enjoys a renaissance at Ship's Inn simply by being infused with the sweet, crunchy taste of fennel. Mark catches the restaurant's meaty cod off Nantucket, and he serves the white, almost translucent fish seared, with an Alsatian-inspired accompaniment of savoy cabbage, cider, and capers.

Mark's cooking is clearly the culmination of a lifelong passion. As a child, he was one of those kids who hung around in the kitchen. His mom was a great cook, and he

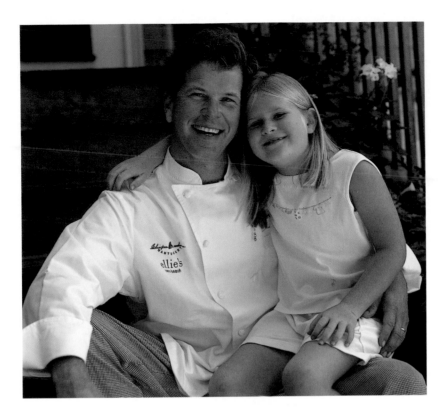

Mark Gottwald and eldest daughter, Grace.

was her "good eater"—always ready to lick the bowl or taste the sauce. This early education, as he was growing up in Richmond, Virginia, was followed by a few restaurant jobs during high school and the three years that he studied at Virginia Tech. Then it dawned on Mark that cooking was really what he wanted to do, and he left college to attend the Baltimore Culinary Arts Institute. From there it was off to France for an advanced program at the famous La Varenne cooking school in Paris.

France was blissful for Mark, not only because of the quality of the cuisine and education that he was exposed to, but also because the raw ingredients were of such high quality. Mark carried this exacting passion for perfect ingredients with him when he went on to work at Le Cirque in New York with Alain Sailhac. Mark was quickly promoted through the ranks, eventually becoming the *poissonier* (fish cook) during the three years that he remained in that esteemed kitchen.

When Mark left Le Cirque, he moved out to West Hollywood to work at the famous Spago restaurant with Wolfgang Puck. For a while, the West Coast was the perfect place for this fisherman-chef-cinemaphile. Mark continued to work at a few California restaurants, including Citrus with Michel Richard, and he met a young actress named Ellie. Mark and Ellie moved to Nantucket, where Mark figured he'd be able both to fish and open a restaurant of his very own. When Ship's Inn came on the

SHIP'S INN

167

market in 1990, he bought it and set about making his dream a reality.

What is now a lively restaurant and inn was originally built in 1831 as a mansion for whaling captain Obed Starbuck. During the early part of the twentieth century, the rambling wooden building was turned into a boarding house, changing hands several times until 1968, when it was purchased by Howard Jelleme. He leased the restaurant to chef John Krebs and his then wife Joyce and together, the three of them transformed the space into a full-service restaurant for the first time. What is now the cozy bar was once a dim storage room. They opened it up and built the actual bar from a handmade, turn-of-the-century cod dory turned on its side. John Krebs stayed with the restaurant (which became a real favorite with locals) for twenty years before moving on.

The property was sold to Mark in 1990, the year he and Ellie were married. Their first joint effort was in coordinating a complete interior makeover for the inn. Fixing the place up became an ongoing project, and every season there are new improvements. There are twelve guest rooms, tastefully appointed with antiques to fit the old-time-mariner feel of the building's history. Downstairs, below street level, are the restaurant's two dining rooms, with alcoves aplenty for more intimate dining and tall portal-style windows to give the rooms a shiplike feel. In fact, everything about the place has a seaside colonial look, making it easy to know you're dining in the restored home of a grand old Nantucket sea captain.

Cheerful flowered cloths and fine hotel-quality table service add elegant finishing touches.

Mark and Ellie were inspired by the success they had at Ship's Inn and decided to complement their summer efforts with a winter restaurant in Vero Beach, Florida. The restaurant is called Ellie's, and it is literally a continuation of Ship's Inn. The cooks, general manager, and some of the wait staff travel with the Gottwalds to work at both restaurants each year. Chris LeMont is in charge of the day-to-day operation of the kitchen, and Bob Moulder is the general manager at both restaurants and Mark's right-hand man. The traveling staff gives Ship's Inn and Ellie's an admirable continuity from year to year, and having so many competent people whom he can trust has allowed Mark to succeed while stirring several pots at the same time.

Mark is busy, but happy, and he seems to have it all. He loves the sea, and he fishes whenever he wants since there is no shortage of shoreline at either of his homes. He is an inspired professional chef who is able to showcase his innovative cooking in two distinct and wonderful restaurants. And he still has time to spend with his beautiful family, which, after all, is what his life is really all about. If you see him strolling in Nantucket with Ellie and the two girls, you may wonder how he has the time to run his businesses and still look so relaxed. Yet somehow he does, and Nantucket is a richer place thanks to Mark's talent and frequent generosity to the community at large.

MENU

Clams Broiled "Croûte Herbe"

Roquefort and Walnut Terrine
with Asian Pear

Crispy Salmon with Celery Root Purée,
Niçoise Vegetables, and Cabernet Sauce

Banana–Butterscotch Cream Tart
with Kahlúa Chocolate Sauce

Clams Broiled
"Croûte Herbe"

A frozen compound butter, seasoned with fresh herbs, lemon, and a touch of garlic, melts into a decadent sauce for broiled clams.

Serves 8

1 cup (2 sticks) unsalted butter, softened

½ cup salt-free cracker crumbs

½ cup chopped fresh herbs (such as a combination of thyme, chives, and sage)

1 egg yolk

½ teaspoon finely minced garlic

2 to 3 dashes of Tabasco sauce
Finely grated zest of 1 small lemon

½ teaspoon salt, plus additional to taste
Freshly ground black pepper, to taste

1 tablespoon sherry vinegar

½ teaspoon honey

3 tablespoons extra-virgin olive oil

1 tablespoon hazelnut oil

48 medium clams, shucked (see sidebar below)

1 quart mâche, washed and dried

1. In a food processor, combine the butter, cracker crumbs, herbs, egg yolk, ¼ teaspoon of the garlic, Tabasco, and lemon zest and process until smooth. Season with salt and pepper.

2. Roll the butter in a large sheet of plastic wrap into a cylinder with a diameter around the same size as your clams. Freeze for at least 2 hours, or overnight.

3. Whisk together the sherry vinegar, honey, the remaining ¼ teaspoon of garlic, and a pinch of salt and pepper. Slowly drizzle in the olive oil and hazelnut oil, whisking constantly. Taste and correct the seasonings. Set the vinaigrette aside.

Shucking Clams

Scrub the clams with a stiff brush under running water. Hold one clam in your hand with the hinge against the joint of your thumb. Place the side (not the tip) of the clam knife into the crack between the shells on the side of the clam (not the front). Twist the knife to pry open the hinge. Run the knife against the upper shell to detach any clinging meat. Remove and discard the upper shell.

4. Just before serving, preheat the broiler. Arrange the clams on a baking tray. Slice the butter into ⅛-inch-thick coins and place them on the clams. Broil the clams for 3 to 5 minutes, or until the tops are lightly browned.

5. Toss the mâche with enough of the vinaigrette to lightly coat the leaves. To serve, place a small mound of dressed greens in the center of each plate. Arrange the clams in a circle around the greens and serve at once.

Roquefort and Walnut Terrine with Asian Pear

Serves 8

2 large red tomatoes

2 large yellow tomatoes

7 tablespoons extra-virgin olive oil

1 tablespoon chopped fresh basil

1¼ teaspoons minced garlic

Salt and freshly ground black pepper, to taste

1½ pounds Roquefort cheese, cold

1 cup walnuts, roughly chopped

3 dashes of Tabasco sauce

1 tablespoon sherry vinegar

½ teaspoon honey

1 tablespoon hazelnut oil

2 large bunches of arugula, washed and dried

3 Asian pears, sliced

8 slices toasted baguette (optional)

1. Bring a large pot of water to a boil. Fill a bowl with ice water. Plunge the tomatoes into the boiling water for 30 seconds, then use a slotted spoon to transfer them to the ice water to cool. When cool enough to handle, core and peel the tomatoes with a paring knife, then halve and seed them. Place the red tomatoes in one bowl and the yellow tomatoes in another bowl.

2. In a small bowl, whisk together 4 tablespoons of the olive oil, the basil, 1 teaspoon of the garlic, and salt and pepper. Pour half the mixture over the red tomatoes and half over the yellow. Toss gently to combine. Let the tomatoes marinate for 30 minutes to 1 hour.

3. Meanwhile, in a bowl, gently mash together the cheese, nuts, and Tabasco, taking care not to overmix.

4. Line a 5-liquid-cup-capacity terrine or a 9-inch loaf pan with plastic wrap, leaving a good amount hanging over the edges. Using a spatula, very firmly press half of the cheese mixture into the terrine. Flatten the marinated tomatoes with the side of a knife, then press a thin layer of red, then yellow tomatoes on top of the cheese. If the tomatoes are watery, blot them with a towel first. Carefully spread the remaining cheese on top and press down hard. Bring up the sides of the plastic to cover the terrine and refrigerate overnight, or for up to 4 days.

5. In a small bowl, whisk together the sherry vinegar, honey, the remaining 1/4 teaspoon of garlic, and a pinch of salt and pepper. Slowly drizzle in the hazelnut oil and the remaining 3 tablespoons of olive oil, whisking constantly. Taste and correct the seasonings. Toss the arugula with enough of the vinaigrette to lightly coat the leaves.

6. Unmold the terrine, removing the plastic wrap, and slice it using a very sharp knife dipped in hot water. To serve, place a slice of terrine on each plate. Place a small mound of greens next to the terrine and arrange the pear slices in two fans on either side. Serve with toasted baguette, if desired.

Crispy Salmon with Celery Root Purée, Niçoise Vegetables, and Cabernet Sauce

Serves 8

FOR THE CABERNET SAUCE

- 3 cups good cabernet wine
- 1 cup beef broth
- 8 tablespoons (1 stick) unsalted butter, cubed
- Salt, to taste

FOR THE PURÉE

- 1 large celery root, peeled
- 3 large baking potatoes
- 1 cup plus 1 tablespoon heavy cream
- 2 tablespoons unsalted butter
- Salt, to taste

FOR THE NIÇOISE VEGETABLES

- 3 medium zucchini, sliced ⅛ inch thick
- 4 medium yellow squash, sliced ⅛ inch thick
- 4 plum tomatoes, sliced ⅛ inch thick
- 2 tablespoons extra-virgin olive oil
- 1 teaspoon fresh thyme leaves
- 2 teaspoons minced garlic
- Salt and freshly ground black pepper, to taste
- Freshly grated Parmesan cheese, to taste

FOR THE SALMON

- Eight 7-ounce salmon fillets (each 1½ inches thick), skin on
- Salt, to taste
- ⅓ cup extra-virgin olive oil
- 3 tablespoons unsalted butter

1. To make the sauce, in a saucepan over high heat, simmer the wine and beef broth until only about ⅓ cup remains, about 20 to 25 minutes. Reduce the heat to very low and gradually whisk in the butter, piece by piece, until the sauce is smooth and satiny. Sea-

son with salt. Cover the sauce to keep warm, or gently reheat before serving, taking care not to let the sauce come to a boil.

2. To make the purée, preheat the oven to 400°F. Wrap the celery root in foil. Wrap the potatoes in another piece of foil. Bake the vegetables until very tender, about 45 minutes to 1 hour. (Leave the oven on.) When cool enough to handle, peel and cube the potatoes. In a blender or food processor, purée the celery root.

3. In a saucepan over medium heat, combine the celery root purée and 1 cup of the cream and simmer for 5 or 6 minutes, or until most of the cream has boiled away.

4. Pass the cooked potatoes through a food mill or potato ricer directly into the celery mixture. (Alternately, mash the potatoes with a potato masher.) Stir in the remaining tablespoon of cream, the butter, and salt. Cover to keep warm.

5. For the niçoise vegetables, oil a baking sheet and arrange the sliced vegetables in overlapping rows, alternating the slices. Brush the vegetables with olive oil and sprinkle with the thyme, garlic, salt, pepper, and Parmesan cheese. Bake for 5 minutes, or until golden brown around the edges.

6. Meanwhile, prepare the fish. Season the fish on both sides with salt. In a large sauté pan over high heat, combine the oil and butter and heat until the foam subsides. Add the fillets, skin side down, giving the pan a shake so the fish won't stick to the bottom. After 1 minute reduce the heat to medium-low and cook for 8 to 9 minutes, until the skin is very brown and crisp. Flip and cook on the other side for 1 minute more. The fish should be firm to the touch and just a little pink in the center.

7. To serve, spoon some sauce in the center of a plate. Place the salmon, skin side up, on top of the sauce. Place some of the vegetables and a large spoonful of purée on either side of the salmon and serve immediately.

Banana–Butterscotch Cream Tart with Kahlúa Chocolate Sauce

If you have individual three-inch tart pans, feel free to use those instead of one large tart pan. It makes for a very elegant presentation. If you don't normally cook with salted butter and haven't any on hand, substitute sweet butter and add a pinch of salt.

Serves 8

FOR THE CRUST

8 tablespoons (1 stick) salted butter, softened

¼ cup (2 ounces) cream cheese

1¼ cups all-purpose flour

2 to 3 tablespoons water

FOR THE PASTRY CREAM

2 large eggs

2 tablespoons cornstarch

2 cups half-and-half

¾ cup light brown sugar

1 tablespoon salted butter

FOR THE CHOCOLATE SAUCE

3 ounces bittersweet chocolate, chopped

⅓ cup heavy cream

1 tablespoon Kahlúa

FOR THE BANANAS

4 firm bananas, sliced ¼ inch thick on the bias

¼ cup granulated sugar

1. To make the crust, in an electric mixer fitted with the paddle attachment, combine the butter and cream cheese and blend until smooth and creamy. Gradually add the flour and mix just until the dough comes together, adding the water, tablespoon by tablespoon, until the dough is smooth. Form the dough into a disk, wrap in plastic, and chill until firm, at least 1 hour.

2. Roll out the dough on a well-floured work surface to ⅛ inch thick. Fit the dough into a 10-inch tart pan and prick all over with a fork; chill for 20 minutes, or up to 24 hours.

3. Preheat the oven to 375°F. Line the tart shell with foil or parchment paper and fill with pie weights, dried beans, or rice. Bake the tart for 20 minutes, then remove the foil and weights and bake for 5 to 10 minutes longer, or until the crust is golden brown. Transfer to a wire rack to cool.

4. To prepare the pastry cream, in a bowl, combine the eggs and cornstarch and whisk well. In a saucepan over high heat, combine the half-and-half and brown sugar and bring to a boil. Add about ½ cup of the half-and-half mixture to the egg mixture, whisking constantly. Add the egg mixture to the saucepan and turn the heat to medium-high. Bring to a simmer, then remove from the heat and stir in the butter. Strain the mixture through a fine sieve and let cool. Cover the cream directly with plastic so a skin won't form and chill until thoroughly cold, at least 3 hours.

5. To make the sauce, in a double boiler over simmering, not boiling, water, melt the chocolate. Remove from the heat and whisk in the cream until smooth and blended. Whisk in the Kahlúa and let cool.

6. To make the bananas, preheat the broiler. Butter a baking sheet. On another, unbuttered baking sheet, arrange the banana slices and sprinkle with sugar. Broil the bananas until they caramelize and the sugar is golden brown and bubbly, 1 to 2 minutes. Immediately transfer the banana slices to the buttered sheet and let cool.

7. To serve, spread the pastry cream in the bottom of the tart shell. Decoratively arrange the banana slices on top and drizzle with the chocolate sauce.

STRAIGHT WHARF

HARBOR SQUARE

508-228-4499

SEASON: MAY THROUGH SEPTEMBER

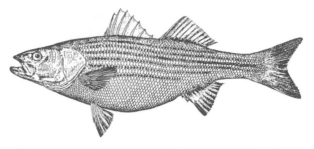

STRAIGHT WHARF RESTAURANT

Astounding as it may seem, when Jock and Laine Gifford opened the Straight Wharf Restaurant in 1976, there were no other upscale seafood restaurants on Nantucket. Nor were there any restaurants on piers surrounded by water and gently lapping waves.

This void bothered Jock, an architect from Boston who both vacationed and occasionally designed on Nantucket. So, when Walter Beinecke, one of Nantucket's foremost real-estate holders, asked him to evaluate a property—a cavernous laundromat on the Straight Wharf—Jock instantly knew that somewhere among the churning washers and driers was a seafood restaurant lying in wait.

Now, more than a quarter of a century later, Straight Wharf remains one of Nantucket's most venerable venues, one that regulars know embodies the spare beauty and elegance—seasoned with a little bit of salt—of Nantucket itself. The Straight Wharf is also a restaurant with distinguished culinary pedigrees that began with Jock's first chef—the noted cookbook author and television personality Marian Morash—and is now safely carried in the hands of Steve and Kate Cavagnaro, also owners of Cavey's, one of the best restaurants in Connecticut.

But to call Straight Wharf a Nantucket institution doesn't really capture its specialness. The best way to truly appreciate it is to go there on a warm summer evening and sip a sunset apéritif on the deck perched over the harbor before commencing your meal. It's a perfect spot to watch the end-of-the-day comings and goings of commercial boats and grand private yachts. On a clear night, just after sunset, the light glows an intense shade of pink, making everyone and everything around you radiant. Libation in one hand and a nibble of the restaurant's signature smoked bluefish pâté in the other, you realize this is one of those moments when the island becomes indelibly magical, enveloping you like the fog over the pier.

Inside, the restaurant abounds with Nantucket charm and eclecticism. Transforming this huge, barnlike space into something welcoming and intimate was a challenge for Jock, however. Instead of fighting the soaring ceilings, he decided to let the airiness of the space set the tone. Then he lined the walls with gray weathered cedar shingles and installed tall windows to face the harbor, creating a room that was an integrated extension of the exterior, as if you were dining on someone's well-appointed patio. Of course, only a very special patio would feature starched white-clothed tables, each set with a unique antique plate in the center, topped by a lit candle beneath a hurricane lamp. To temper the noise level, Jock hung what looked like diaphanous blue cloths from the rafters, but underneath their floating facade were concealed heavy pieces of carpet underlayment to absorb and cushion the sound. Still, when the large room is filled to capacity, as it is almost every night in season, a convivial hum fills the air, imparting an exciting buzz to the refined ambience.

Since Jock had never been in the restaurant business before, he felt that his first venture should be extremely personal, as if the diners were all guests invited into his home. So instead of looking for a professional chef to lead the kitchen, he asked two

of his friends from Boston to be co-chefs. Jock and Laine had enjoyed many extraordinary meals prepared by Marian Morash and Susan Mayer at dinner parties and thought, Why not have them cook for Straight Wharf? After a bit of cajoling, they agreed, cooking together for five years, after which Susan left to be with her family.

During Marian's eleven-year tenure, she helped to literally change the way people ate on Nantucket. Indeed, one reason there weren't any upscale fish restaurants on Nantucket in the 1970s was just that people weren't in the habit of eating a lot of fish. But Marian created an exciting menu emphasizing freshly caught seafood and the cornucopia of just-picked local vegetables. It set the tone for a generation of Nantucket restaurants to come.

When not cooking at Straight Wharf in the summers, Marian remained immersed in the food world, working on an in-

Jock Gifford, Kate Cavagnaro, and Kate's husband, Steve.

spiring tome of recipes, published in 1982 as the *Victory Garden Cookbook*, and hosting a companion PBS television series.

That PBS show was not Marian's first brush with the world of television. For years before, she was the executive chef for Julia Child's PBS shows, and her husband, Russell, was the producer. Marian and Julia became such good friends that one summer, Julia came to the island and worked in the restaurant for a few days. Julia had never worked in a restaurant kitchen before and wanted to experience it firsthand. She worked the line in each station, and had a marvelous time doing it. Although Jock and Marian didn't advertise that Julia was visiting, word escaped, and to this day people still talk about the time Julia Child cooked at Straight Wharf.

As rewarding as restaurant work is, it is also exhausting, and after eleven years of working fourteen-hour days on Nantucket during the summer, Marian left the helm. Sarah O'Neill, her sous-chef, took over and carried on the tradition for another nine years. After she left—now twenty years later—it was time for some new blood.

While Jock and Laine were pondering the situation at Straight Wharf, another couple, Steve and Kate Cavagnaro, were pondering it too, but from a different side. Unlike Jock and Marian, who had been amateurs when Straight Wharf opened, Steve and Kate had years of experience in the restaurant business. In fact, the couple already owned the highly successful Cavey's

in Manchester, Connecticut. This restaurant had been in Steve's family for three generations and Steve grew up lending a hand whenever he was needed. Although he went to college thinking he'd become an engineer, after graduation his foodie notions got the best of him and that love, combined with a strong sense of family responsibility, made him decide to get involved with the business. He and his wife, Kate, took over Cavey's and modernized Steve's grandmother's "continental" Italian menu into something more regional, stressing the foods of his grandparents' native Genoa and the Mediterranean. He also added a small French restaurant in the downstairs, which is immensely popular.

At the same time, the couple began spending their summer vacations on Nantucket and dreaming that someday the island could become their part-time home.

Of course, as any Nantucket enthusiast

can attest, if you were vacationing here in the 1970s and '80s, you most likely were eating a fair share of meals at Straight Wharf. Kate and Steve were no exceptions, adoring the creative food and atmosphere and returning year after year.

In the mid-1990s, the Cavagnaros got serious about making Nantucket their summer home and began looking for a location to open a seasonal restaurant. Nantucket, with its surfeit of both adventurous diners and stellar ingredients, could be completely compatible with what Steve was doing at Cavey's. Opening another venue began to make more and more sense.

But finding a suitable spot for a restaurant on the island wasn't easy. After much looking, Steve and Kate decided to approach Jock at Straight Wharf to see if they could become partners. The couple knew it was a long shot, but Jock and the Cavagnaros hit it off and were able to make a deal: Jock was to remain an active partner, but he agreed to step back and let Kate and Steve revamp the restaurant in their own style. In 1996, the Cavagnaros had their first season at Straight Wharf, and each year has been better than the last. But it's still an evolving process as Kate and Steve continue to put their own stamp on things while still catering to their inherited loyal regulars.

Now, the menu at Straight Wharf is infused with the same Mediterranean essence and vibrant flavors of Cavey's, though the focus is heavy on seafood. Steve, who admits to being a little obsessed with ingredients, has the best of both worlds in combining what he can get locally in Connecticut with the ocean's abundance on Nantucket. Everything is made on premises, even the vinegar. In addition, Steve and Kate have also revitalized the wine program at the restaurant, employing a full-time wine steward. The list reflects Steve's love and knowledge of Italian wines, and he has stocked plenty of wonderful, rare bottles from smaller producers along with the requisite big names.

The kind of independence and daring that Kate and Steve showed when they took over Straight Wharf is remarkable, and even more so when you realize how well their innovations work. Although the menu is entirely their own, it does carry on, and indeed has built upon, Marian's basic philosophy of fresh, creative, and seasonal seafood. The Cavagnaros kept only one dish from the old Straight Wharf: the smoked bluefish pâté that greets you and graces the table. Kate and Steve knew that it wouldn't be right to continue to call the place the Straight Wharf without the salty, smoky, creamy spread and chunks of bread that have kicked off each and every memorable meal since the restaurant opened. It's the symbol that underscores the spirit of hospitality and creativity that Straight Wharf brought to the island and that the Cavagnaros have managed to carry into the new millennium.

MENU

Marian Morash's Smoked Bluefish Pâté

Polenta-Crusted Sea Scallops
with Corn and Oyster Sauce

Tomatoes Méditerranée with Baby Arugula
and Goat Cheese Croque Monsieur

Moroccan-Spiced Wild Striped Bass
with Couscous and Minted Cucumber

Crème Brûlée Napoleon

Marian Morash's
Smoked Bluefish Pâté

Serves 6 to 8

⅓ lb. smoked bluefish

1 lb. cream cheese, at room temperature

1½ cups chopped parsley

½ cup chopped red onions

¼ cup fresh lemon juice

Salt and freshly ground black pepper, to taste

1. Using a small knife, carefully remove the skin, bones, and any dark flesh from the fish and flake it into small pieces.

2. Put the cream cheese in the bowl of an electric mixer and beat it with the paddle attachment to soften it (alternately, use a wooden spoon). Add the bluefish and mix well. Add the parsley, onions, and lemon juice and beat until well combined. Season with salt and freshly ground pepper.

3. Spoon the mixture into a serving dish and refrigerate, covered, until ready to serve or for at least 1 hour. Serve with melba rounds or toasted thin rounds of French bread or sourdough baguettes.

Polenta-Crusted Sea Scallops with Corn and Oyster Sauce

Steve uses only perfectly fresh diver-caught scallops at the restaurant, and if you use them, they will make this already delightful dish into something even more impressive. Just note that fresh scallops take longer to cook through than frozen ones, so watch your scallops closely when cooking them. They are done when they hover between translucent and opaque.

Serves 6

1 cup chicken stock

½ cup quick-cooking polenta

¼ cup milk

2 tablespoons heavy cream

2 tablespoons plus 2 teaspoons unsalted butter

1 heaping teaspoon minced scallion

¼ teaspoon salt, plus more to taste

2 tablespoons freshly grated Parmesan cheese, preferably Parmigiano-Reggiano

⅓ cup all-purpose flour

6 large (U10) diver scallops

Freshly ground black pepper, to taste

3 tablespoons canola oil

2 tablespoons minced leek (white part only)

6 tablespoons diced leek (white part only)

¾ cup raw corn kernels, cut from the cob

3 oysters, shucked

¼ teaspoon verjus (see Note)

Minced fresh chives, for garnish

1. In a medium saucepan, bring the stock to a boil. Add the polenta in a thin stream and stir to avoid clumping. When the mixture returns to a simmer, add the milk, cream, 2 tablespoons of the butter, scallion, and salt; continue simmering for 5 to 7 minutes, or until the polenta is thick and creamy. Blend in the Parmesan and scrape the polenta out ¼ inch thick onto a sheet pan lined with parchment or waxed paper. Chill the polenta until cold and solid, about 1 hour.

2. Preheat the oven to 400°F. Place the flour in a shallow dish. Using a knife or cookie cutter, cut out rounds of polenta that are approximately the same size as the scallops. Dredge the scallops in flour lightly and season with salt and pepper on both sides. Press a round of polenta on top of each scallop and set aside.

3. In a large, oven-proof sauté pan, heat the canola oil over high heat. Place the scallops in the pan, polenta side down, and cook until the polenta is browned, about 1 minute. Flip the scallops and sear until golden, about 30 seconds. Transfer the pan to the oven and roast until the scallops are just cooked through, about 3 to 4 minutes for medium-rare.

4. In a small saucepan, melt the remaining 2 teaspoons of butter over medium heat. Add the minced leek and cook for 1 to 2 minutes, until softened. Add the diced leek and ¼ cup of the corn and cook for 2 minutes longer.

5. In a food processor, purée the oysters and their liquor with the remaining ½ cup of corn. If necessary, thin the mixture with a little water to get a smooth purée. Strain the sauce directly into the sauté pan with the leek and mix well. Gently reheat the sauce, then stir in the verjus and seasonings to taste.

6. Spoon the sauce onto each plate, top with a scallop, and sprinkle with chives. Serve at once.

Note: Verjus is the juice pressed from unripe grapes. It has a tart flavor that is less acidic than vinegar, though the two are often used similarly. Verjus is available in specialty food shops, but if you can't find it, substitute lemon juice.

Tomatoes Méditerranée with Baby Arugula and Goat Cheese Croque Monsieur

For this and all his salads, Steve makes his own red wine vinegar in wine barrels. It has an intense fruity flavor that can be somewhat duplicated by using any top-quality red wine vinegar.

To remove bitterness from red onion, Steve likes to rinse it three times in cold water, squeezing and draining after each rinse.

Serves 6 to 8

1 cup olive oil

1 small bunch of basil, washed and dried

1 sheet phyllo dough, thawed

3 tablespoons unsalted butter, melted

3 ounces soft fresh goat cheese

½ cup finely diced red onion

1 tablespoon red wine vinegar

2 small celery stalks, trimmed and diced

¼ cup diced green bell pepper

¼ cup diced red bell pepper

2 black dry-cured Greek olives, pitted and chopped

1 marinated white anchovy fillet or 1 salted anchovy (washed and boned), or 1 oil-packed anchovy fillet, mashed

Sea salt and freshly ground black pepper, to taste

6 tablespoons extra-virgin olive oil

2 tablespoons fresh lemon juice

2 tablespoons balsamic vinegar

2 bunches of arugula, trimmed, washed, and dried

1 large red tomato, cored and sliced

1. Prepare the basil oil 2 days ahead of time. In a small saucepan, slowly heat the oil until it just begins to bubble around the edges (180°F), then turn off the heat and add all but one large leaf of the basil. Let the oil steep for 48 hours at room temperature. Strain and discard the solids.

2. To make the croque monsieur, slice the phyllo sheet in half. Butter one half, then layer the other half on top and butter the top lightly. Cut the phyllo into 1-by-3-inch strips. Lay one strip horizontally on a work surface. Top with another strip vertically to make a cross. Place a half-ounce piece of cheese in the center of the cross, then fold in the left side and then the right side of the phyllo to cover the cheese, patting it down well. Fold

up the top and bottom to make a neat little square. Set aside. (These will keep for up to 1 week, well wrapped in the refrigerator.)

3. In a bowl, combine the onion and vinegar and let sit for 10 minutes, stirring a couple of times. Add the celery, bell peppers, and olives and stir to combine well. Add the mashed anchovy a little at a time to taste. Add 1 tablespoon of the basil oil and season with salt and pepper.

4. Chop the remaining basil leaf and reserve. In a small bowl, whisk together the extra-virgin olive oil, lemon juice, and vinegar. Dress the arugula with the vinaigrette and divide it among serving plates; surround the greens with the tomato slices. Season the tomato with salt and pepper. Spoon 1 to 2 tablespoons of the onion mixture on top of the tomatoes and garnish with the chopped basil.

5. Just before serving, heat the remaining butter in a nonstick pan and brown the phyllo packages on both sides, about 2 minutes total. Add to the plate and drizzle lightly with more basil oil.

Moroccan-Spiced Wild Striped Bass with Couscous and Minted Cucumber

Steve strongly recommends grinding whole spices instead of using preground. He finds the flavor of the freshly ground spices to be much more intense. Before grinding whole spices, it's best to toast them in a hot, dry skillet for a minute or two. Then grind them in a coffee grinder or pound them in a mortar.

Serves 6 to 8

FOR THE DICED TOMATOES

3 plum tomatoes

FOR THE HARISSA

2 tablespoons olive oil

⅓ cup minced onion

2 garlic cloves, minced

1 small hot red pepper (Thai chili or serrano), seeded and minced

1 teaspoon ground cumin

½ teaspoon ground coriander

1 roasted red bell pepper, peeled, seeded, and chopped (see sidebar, page 148)

Diced tomatoes (see above)

Grated zest of 1 lemon

Salt and freshly ground black pepper, to taste

FOR THE CUCUMBER SALAD

1 English cucumber, peeled, halved lengthwise, seeded, and thinly sliced

1 teaspoon coarse salt

½ teaspoon sugar

10 fresh mint leaves, chopped

Splash of wine vinegar, to taste

Salt and freshly ground black pepper, to taste

1½ cups couscous

1½ cups chicken stock

2 tablespoons grapeseed oil

⅛ teaspoon sesame oil

2 garlic cloves, minced

1 teaspoon minced peeled ginger

½ cup small-diced onion

¼ cup small-diced celery

¼ cup small-diced carrot

¼ cup small-diced red bell pepper

¼ cup small-diced yellow bell pepper

¼ cup small-diced zucchini

Diced tomatoes (see above)

¼ cup diced cucumber

¼ cup champagne grapes (see Note, page 192)

1 scallion, cleaned, trimmed, and chopped

1 teaspoon chopped fresh mint leaves

½ teaspoon fresh lemon juice

½ teaspoon chopped preserved lemon (optional)

⅜ teaspoon curry powder

⅜ teaspoon ground cumin

Pinch of ground cinnamon

Salt and freshly ground black pepper, to taste

6 striped bass fillets (about 6 ounces each), skin on

Salt and freshly ground black pepper, to taste

2 tablespoons canola oil

1. For the tomatoes, bring a small pot of water to a boil. Fill a bowl with ice water. Plunge the tomatoes into the boiling water for 30 seconds, then use a slotted spoon to transfer to the ice water to cool. When cool enough to handle, core and peel the tomatoes with a paring knife, then halve and seed them. Cut them into ¼-inch dice and reserve.

2. To make the harissa, heat the olive oil in a sauté pan over low heat. Add the onion and garlic and sauté until they become transparent, about 2 minutes. Add the hot red pepper, cumin, and coriander and sauté for 1 minute longer. Add the roasted bell pepper and about two thirds of the diced tomatoes and cook over low heat, stirring occasionally, until thick and jamlike, about 20 minutes. Transfer the sauce to a blender or food processor, add the lemon zest and salt and pepper, and purée. To achieve a ketchup-like consistency, thin the sauce with water if necessary.

3. To prepare the cucumber salad, in a bowl, toss together the cucumber, salt, and sugar and let sit for 30 minutes. Strain and discard the liquid and add the mint, vinegar, and seasonings. Set aside.

4. Prepare the couscous with the chicken stock according to the package directions and set aside. Heat the oils in a sauté pan over high heat. Add the garlic and ginger and cook until they just begin to color, about 2 minutes. Add the onion, celery, and carrot and sauté for about 1 minute longer. Add the peppers and zucchini and sauté for another minute. Add the couscous to the pan and mix well, heating it through. Stir in the remaining diced tomato, cucumber, grapes, scallion, mint leaves, lemon juice, preserved lemon, curry powder, cumin, cinnamon, salt, and pepper and toss to combine.

5. To prepare the bass, preheat the oven to 400°F. Using a sharp knife, score the skin of the bass in a crosshatch pattern. Generously season both sides of the fish with salt and pepper.

6. In a large, heavy skillet, heat the oil over medium heat. Add the fish, skin side down, and sear for 2 1/2 to 3 minutes. Flip the fish and sear 1 to 1 1/2 minutes more. Place the pan in the oven and roast for 3 minutes, or until the fish is just cooked through.

7. To serve, place a mound of couscous on each plate and arrange the fish, skin side up, leaning against the couscous. Place the cucumber salad and a squiggle or dots of harissa around the plate and serve at once.

Note: *If you can't find champagne grapes (tiny red grapes available in specialty produce markets in autumn), you can substitute small seedless red grapes. Simply halve them, then lay them on a baking sheet and dry them in a 200°F. oven for 1 hour.*

Crème Brûlée Napoleon

Steve uses anise hyssop leaves from the herb garden next to the restaurant to lend a faint licorice flavor to the custard. You can use star anise or fennel seeds instead. (Note: The recipe makes extra phyllo squares, which will keep for weeks in a sealed container at room temperature.)

Serves 6

FOR THE CRÈME BRÛLÉE

2¾ cups heavy cream

⅔ cup milk

⅔ cup granulated sugar

1 vanilla bean, split lengthwise and
scraped

1 or 2 anise hyssop flowers or leaves
(or 2 pieces star anise or 1 tablespoon
toasted fennel seed)

8 large egg yolks

FOR THE PHYLLO

4 sheets of phyllo dough

¼ cup melted butter

¼ cup sugar

FOR SERVING

18 ripe figs, halved (Black Mission if
possible)

¼ cup light brown sugar

3 tablespoons superfine sugar

1. To make the crème brûlée, preheat the oven to 325°F. In a medium saucepan, bring the cream, milk, ⅓ cup of the sugar, the vanilla bean scrapings and pod, and anise hyssop to a simmer. In a large bowl, whisk together the remaining ⅓ cup of sugar with the egg yolks. Gradually pour a little of the hot cream into the yolk mixture, stirring constantly, then pour in the remaining cream mixture, continuing to stir constantly. Allow the mixture to cool for 10 minutes, then strain.

2. Pour the mixture into a nonreactive 8-by-8-inch baking dish (glass, stainless steel, or nonstick coated metal). Set the baking dish in a larger baking dish or on top of a jelly-roll pan and fill the larger pan with very hot water. Ideally, the water should come halfway up the sides of the baking dish, but if using a jelly-roll pan, fill it as high as pos-

sible. Bake the custard until the center is just set, 20 to 40 minutes (metal pans take less time than glass). Remove the baking dish from the water bath and transfer to a wire rack to cool. Cover the custard with plastic wrap placed directly on its surface and chill until firm, at least 4 hours or overnight.

3. To prepare the phyllo, preheat the oven to 375°F. Lay the first sheet of phyllo on a baking sheet. Brush with butter and sprinkle with one third of the sugar. Layer on the second sheet and repeat with more butter and sugar. Repeat a third time and top with the last sheet of phyllo. Cut the phyllo into 20 rectangles, then cut each rectangle along the diagonal to form 2 triangles. Bake the phyllo until browned and crisp, about 10 minutes, then transfer the pan to a wire rack to cool.

4. Just before serving, preheat the broiler. Arrange the figs on a pan, cut side up. Sprinkle with the brown sugar and broil until the sugar has melted and caramelized, 1 to 2 minutes. Set aside.

5. Cut the custard into 6 rectangles and carefully transfer them with a spatula to a baking sheet. Sprinkle the superfine sugar over the tops. Broil the custards until the top caramelizes, about 1 to 1½ minutes. Watch carefully so they do not burn.

6. To serve, place a phyllo triangle on a plate and top with a crème brûlée. Lean two more phyllo triangles next to the crème brûlée and place three figs around the edges of the plate. Repeat with the remaining crème brûlées and figs and serve at once.

TOPPER'S

THE WAUWINET INN

WAUWINET ROAD

508-228-0145

WWW.WAUWINET.COM/DINING

SEASON: MAY THROUGH OCTOBER

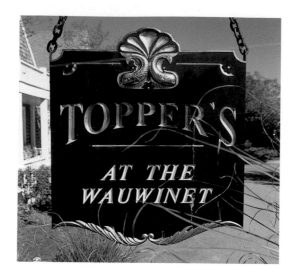

You might have to travel to the far ends of the earth to find a landscape this breathtaking. As you stand on the beach in front of the Wauwinet Inn and turn your head left or right, you'll simply see spectacular untouched shore punctuated by tangled, billowing tufts of beach grass. Look ahead, and you're face-to-face with the choppy blue embrace of the harbor. All you hear is the whistle of the wind and the high-pitched cry of gulls. It really does feel as if you're on the outer limits of the world—until you look behind you. For there stands the Wauwinet, arguably Nantucket's grandest inn.

Located on a strip of sandy land between the Atlantic Ocean and Nantucket Sound at the northeast end of the island, the Wauwinet, the island's only Relais et Châteaux establishment, is set in a spot as romantic as it is sublime. In loyal Nantucket style, the inn exudes an understated cottage elegance, from its weathered cedar-shingled exterior to the pickled-pine floors of the interior.

Topper's, the hotel's restaurant, is similarly soigné. It was named for the owners' dog, who seems equally at home bounding about the naturally landscaped property or curled up in front of one of the inn's fireplaces on a brisk fall night. Originally called the Wauwinet House, it opened as a restaurant in the mid-nineteenth century serving "shore dinners" to patrons arriving exclusively by boat to this relatively remote part of the island. In 1876, when the Wauwinet House added guest rooms and cottages, it was described as "just what has been needed—a beach house, a place where a party can feel at home and enjoy a true Nantucket clambake."

By 1934, the property had grown to three floors with beds for sixty guests, and in 1976 it celebrated its one hundredth anniversary of serving the island. Ten years later, the property was purchased by Bostonians Stephen and Jill Karp. They undertook a twenty-month, three-million-dollar renovation, rebuilding the Wauwinet from the foundations up. This included a completely new kitchen and Topper's restaurant. Opening an outstanding restaurant on a restaurant-conscious island was part of the Karps' vision, and with Topper's, they fulfilled it with aplomb.

Those who relish the journey as much as the destination will be sure to arrive at Topper's by boat, while others may drive fifteen minutes from town by car. The hotel's sporty little launch leaves the Straight Wharf dock each evening during peak season, transporting you from the hustle and bustle of town out across the lapping waves of Nantucket Sound. You can relax and sip a glass of champagne as you glide by the waterfront mansions of Quaise and Pocomo, watching the pink light of dusk reflect on the water. When you arrive at the Wauwinet's private dock forty-five minutes later, your hair slightly tousled and salt-sprayed, the restaurant is just a stroll across the hotel's lush green lawn.

Be sure to begin your evening in Topper's muraled bar, where martinis arrive in crystal pitchers on graceful samovar trays. Or choose a wine from the restaurant's outstanding 20,000-bottle cellar. When you're ready for dinner, dine al fresco on the terrace or in one of two dining rooms where chintz, gingham, and fresh flowers abound

and surround. Innkeeper Debbie Cleveland has seen to every detail. Once seated, prepare yourself for an exceptionally fine dining experience. In true "grand hotel" fashion, the service is somewhat formal: plates are delivered to table on domed sterling pendulum plate carriers, the flatware has an imposing heft, and the glassware is Austrian crystal. The food, however, is far from the standard hotel fare.

Executive chef Chris Freeman's regional, contemporary American cuisine focuses on fresh local ingredients used in innovative combinations, with a mind to simplicity and purity. The tuna tartare appetizer showcases an unadorned yellowfin tuna steak, presented with pickled vegetables and carrot-ginger sauce. Fish and seafood feature prominently, of course, but the menu also includes entrées such as herbed chicken paired with the earthy flavors of an eggplant-and-wild-mushroom hash, a perfect filet mignon, and a vegetarian option such as the combination of delicate spring vegetables with the surprise crunch of quinoa and wheat berries. All of the pastries, desserts, ice creams, sorbets, and breads are made on the premises. This fine-tuned cuisine is a perfect extension of the exquisite surroundings.

Chris and Topper's are a good fit. Everything about his history before taking the reins from Peter Wallace in 1997 seems to have prepared him for the job. He grew up in coastal Kennebunkport, Maine, and through high school he held summer

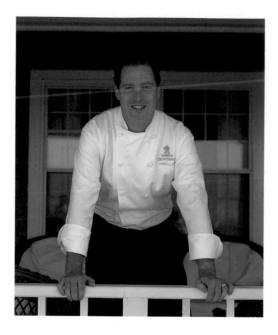

Chef Chris Freeman.

restaurant jobs, moving from dishwasher to prep cook at various restaurants in the resort community. Things would close down during the quiet winters, and Chris became accustomed to the rhythm of a seasonal business.

Though he knew at the time that a future as a chef was calling him, when Chris graduated from high school in the early 1980s, culinary school and the chef's career weren't considered on par with a college education and a more "traditional" profession. He gave it a shot for a year as an engineering major, but his heart wasn't in it. In 1984 he finally enrolled in the Culinary Institute of America. It was during a winter externship at Stowe, Vermont, that Chris began to realize that the rhythms of resort life were for him. He appreciates a clientele that is there primarily to enjoy themselves, to step away from the daily grind and indulge a little.

Chris's most formative education began when he was hired at a resort restaurant in the U.S. Virgin Islands. There, he met chef John Farnsworth, the mentor whom he would accompany to Hawaii, then Connecticut, before taking off on his own. At Topper's, Chris continues to draw on the discoveries he made in Hawaii, subtly adding hints of Pacific Rim flavors to his summer sauces and relishes and coaxing the maximum flavor from the freshest ingredients, rather than covering them up with fancy cream- or butter-laden sauces.

Today, Chris continues developing his techniques, combining seasonal ingredients and regional foods with a focus on simplicity. "Once you have provided the best product, once you are confident in your cooking methods, then," according to Chris's philosophy, "it is a matter of tasting each element and allowing its natural complexity to come through."

In every way, working at Topper's has turned out to be Chris's dream job. Putting a year's worth of work into a six-month season gives him some down time, as well as the chance to travel with his wife, Heather, to places like Napa, Sonoma, and France, and to dine out and concoct new recipes. But in all his touring, he is never tempted to move away from Nantucket, for the island's landscapes, people, and native foods remain an endless and constant source of inspiration. "Every time I come back," he marvels, "it always feels special."

MENU

Warm Oysters with Fennel,
Apples, and Curry

Micro Greens with Seckel Pears,
Buttermilk Blue Cheese, Toasted Pecans,
and Cider Vinaigrette

Grilled Yellowfin Tuna with Baby White
Lima Bean Succotash and Jonah Crab

Pumpkin Financiers

Warm Oysters with Fennel, Apples, and Curry

Serves 4

24 oysters, preferably large, cold-water
    type

4 tablespoons (½ stick) unsalted butter

¼ cup chopped shallot

1½ tablespoons sweet curry powder

½ tablespoon hot curry powder

1 cup white wine

4 apples, such as Rome or Macintosh

¼ cup apple juice

¼ cup crème fraîche

¼ cup chopped fennel

Salt and freshly ground black pepper,
    to taste

Chopped chives, for garnish

Salmon caviar, for garnish

Baguette, for serving

1. Scrub the oyster shells, and shuck, straining the liquid through a cheesecloth-lined sieve. Reserve the liquid and discard the shells.

2. In a medium saucepan over medium-low heat, melt 2 tablespoons of the butter and sauté the shallot, stirring, until translucent, about 2 to 3 minutes. Stir in the curry powders and sauté for 1 minute more. Pour the white wine into the pan, raise the heat to medium-high, and simmer the mixture until it is reduced by half.

3. Dice 3 of the apples into 1-inch cubes, leaving the skin on. Peel the remaining apple, chop, and set aside. Add the large apple cubes and apple juice to the curry mixture, bring to a simmer, and cook until the apples are soft, about 10 minutes. Transfer the mixture to a blender or food processor, add 1 tablespoon of the butter, the oyster juice, and crème fraîche, and blend well.

4. Heat the remaining tablespoon of butter in a large saucepan over medium-high heat and cook the fennel and chopped apple, stirring, for 1 minute. Add the curry sauce and bring it to a simmer. Then add the oysters and swirl them in the pan to coat with sauce. Season with salt and pepper and simmer gently for 1 minute, or until the sides of the oysters begin to curl.

5. To serve, spoon 6 oysters into each bowl and top with the sauce, chopped chives, and salmon caviar. Serve with a sliced baguette.

Micro Greens with Seckel Pears, Buttermilk Blue Cheese, Toasted Pecans, and Cider Vinaigrette

This delightful salad can be made with any flavorful baby greens, such as mâche, mizuna, arugula, watercress, or tatsoi. Chris is careful not to overdress his greens, but he does like to add generous grindings of sea salt and fresh pepper at the end.

Serves 4

½ cup pecan halves

2 tablespoons cider vinegar

1 tablespoon chopped shallots

Salt and freshly ground black pepper, to taste

7 tablespoons extra-virgin olive oil

1 quart baby salad greens, washed and dried

4 Seckel pears, quartered, cored, and sliced

¼ pound buttermilk blue cheese, crumbled

1. Preheat the oven to 350°F. Spread the pecans out on a baking sheet and toast them in the oven until they smell nutty, 7 to 10 minutes. Stir the pecans once or twice as they toast. Transfer the pan to a wire rack to cool.

2. In a small bowl, whisk together the vinegar, shallots, and salt and pepper. Slowly drizzle in the oil, whisking. Taste and correct the seasonings.

3. In a large bowl, toss together the greens, pears, cheese, and dressing. Taste and add more salt and pepper if necessary. Sprinkle the nuts on top and serve immediately.

Grilled Yellowfin Tuna with Baby White Lima Bean Succotash and Jonah Crab

Serves 6

1½ cups fresh corn kernels
 Salt
 1 cup dried lima beans, cooked, or 3 cups cooked lima beans (drained and rinsed if canned)
 1 small onion, chopped
 2 celery stalks, chopped
 1 carrot, peeled and chopped
 6 slices pancetta (2 ounces total)
 1 large tomato
 2 tablespoons olive oil

 1 tablespoon chopped shallot
 ½ cup shelled fresh fava beans or thawed frozen fava beans, peeled
 1 tablespoon chopped fresh flat-leaf parsley
 1 tablespoon chopped fresh chives
 Six 6-ounce yellowfin tuna steaks
 Freshly ground black pepper, to taste
 6 ounces cooked Jonah crabmeat (see sidebar), or lump crabmeat

1. Fill a bowl with ice water. In a large pot of boiling water over medium-high heat, cook the corn kernels with a generous pinch of salt for 1 minute. Drain, then transfer the kernels to the ice water to stop the cooking process. Drain again and set aside.

2. In a large saucepan over medium heat, combine the lima beans, onion, celery, and carrot in just enough water to cover. Simmer the mixture until the vegetables are very soft, about 20 minutes. Drain, reserving the cooking liquid. In a blender, purée 1 cup of the lima beans and vegetables with the cooking liquid and set aside.

3. Preheat the oven to 400°F. Arrange the slices of pancetta on a baking sheet between 2 pieces of parchment paper. Place another baking sheet on top to weigh down the slices. Bake until crisp, about 10 to 12 minutes. Transfer the pancetta to a wire rack to cool.

4. Fill a bowl with ice water. Bring a large pot of water to a boil. Add the tomato and blanch for 10 seconds, then drain and plunge into the ice water to cool. Core the tomato and slide it from its skin; quarter and remove the seeds. Dice the tomato into 1-inch pieces.

5. Meanwhile, in a saucepan, heat 1 tablespoon of the oil over medium heat. Add the shallot and sauté until translucent, about 2 to 3 minutes. Stir in the fava beans, tomato, whole bean–vegetable mixture, corn, parsley, and chives. Add just enough of the bean-vegetable purée to coat all the vegetables (about 1 cup). Stir the mixture until it is heated through, about 2 minutes. Set aside and keep warm.

6. Heat a cast-iron grill over high heat until very hot. Brush the tuna steaks with oil, then sprinkle with salt and pepper. Grill the steaks until medium-rare, about 45 seconds to 2 minutes per side depending on the heat of the grill and the thickness of the steaks.

7. To serve, place the bean mixture in the center of the plate, arrange a tuna steak on top, and garnish with crabmeat and pancetta.

Jonah Crabs

Jonah crabs can be found in Spanish and Chinese markets, but if your fishmonger does not offer them, the more expensive Dungeness crab can be used instead (or lump crabmeat picked clean). Estimate that a whole crab will weigh 4 to 7 times as much as the meat it yields, so roughly 2 pounds of crabs will yield 6 ounces of crabmeat. If you buy uncooked crabs, scrub them well with water and a brush, then plunge them into boiling water and cook for 8 to 10 minutes, until their shells have gone from brown to red. Drain the crabs and, when they are cool enough, hold the legs down with one hand while prying the top shell away with the other. Remove and discard the exposed gills from either side of the body, as well as the front section (the mouth) and the white intestines. Turn the crab over and pull away the end portion (the apron); discard it. Pull the legs off at the base and use a mallet or rolling pin to crack them, then use a crab pick to take the meat from the legs. Quarter the crab's body to pick it clean. Check to ensure that there are no fragments of shell left in the crabmeat before you use it.

Pumpkin Financiers

Serves 8 to 10

4 large egg whites

½ cup sugar

7 tablespoons unsalted butter

½ cup pumpkin purée (canned is fine)

⅔ cup cake flour

⅔ cup almond flour

¼ teaspoon ground nutmeg

¼ teaspoon ground cinnamon

Vanilla ice cream or whipped cream, for serving

1. Preheat the oven to 425°F. In the bowl of an electric mixer fitted with the whisk attachment, whip the egg whites until foamy. Add 2 tablespoons of the sugar and continue to whip until they form stiff peaks.

2. In a small saucepan over medium heat, melt the butter and let it cook, without stirring, until the white milk solids fall to the bottom of the pan and turn brown, about 5 minutes. Strain through a fine sieve and discard the solids.

3. In a small bowl, mix together the pumpkin, remaining 6 tablespoons of sugar, and browned butter. In a medium bowl, sift together the cake flour, almond flour, nutmeg, and cinnamon. Fold the pumpkin mixture into the egg whites, then fold the dry ingredients into the egg mixture.

4. Pour the batter into individual tart molds or muffin tins coated with nonstick spray, and bake for 12 minutes. Let cool on a wire rack before unmolding. Serve garnished with vanilla ice cream or whipped cream.

21
FEDERAL

21 FEDERAL STREET

508-228-2121

WWW.21FEDERAL.NET

SEASON: APRIL THROUGH DECEMBER

At first glimpse, you might mistake 21 Federal for a stuffy gentlemen's club. The sublimely crafted cherry-wood bar flanked by dining rooms with fireplaces suggests men in impeccably tailored suits imbibing single-malt scotch.

But look again.

Upon a second peek, you'll most certainly want to linger to smell the profusion of freshly picked flowers, bask in the mellow candlelight, and take in the stylish clientele—who, even if they might sometimes sip a single-malt, are anything but staid.

Located in a handsome, 1847 Greek Revival former shipwright's building at the distinguished central address from which it takes its name, 21 Federal epitomizes the best of Nantucket restaurant style. Owner Chick (Charles) Walsh has created a true island bistro—one in which you can eat a terrific homey stew at the bar, and accompany it with an even more terrific $300 bottle of Bordeaux. And you are as likely to find yourself seated next to a vacationing CEO of a major company, such as co-owner Nelson Doubleday, as to a local carpenter. Much of the magic of 21 Federal is that it somehow manages to have an appeal for everyone. No mean feat!

Despite the highly social and occasionally boisterous ambience of the bar, which during holidays and the summer season often overflows into the adjacent dining rooms, the food at 21 Federal is taken seriously. Just like the understated yet painstakingly restored setting, the fare is straightforward by design, top quality without any pretention. As Chick describes it, 21 Federal's philosophy is to use "first-rate ingredients, but not be so fussy that we lose track of what's on the plate."

For example, the chicken—free-range, of course—is perfectly crisp and herbaceous on the outside, juicy on the inside, accompanied by memorably good mashed potatoes and slender asparagus. A grilled aged sirloin comes bistro-style, with a satisfyingly charred, salty exterior, tangles of shoestring potatoes to soak up the juices, and perfectly cooked haricots verts to brighten and balance the plate. It gets more adventurous from there, with much of the menu changing weekly. Seared rare tuna might turn up one week paired with a lemongrass broth and littleneck clams, and the next week with white beans and oregano.

Executive chef Russell Jaehnig is careful not to get carried away by trendy ingredients or techniques, keeping the menu grounded in seasonal, regional foods. In August, salmon may be potato crusted with braised endive and shiitake butter, while the first chill of September inspires another dish altogether in which salmon is paired with a creamy broth of clams and corn, straddling the flavors of summer and fall.

The themes of the weekly menu carry the collective influences of each chef who has worked at 21 Federal over the years. The restaurant's first chef and original partner, Bob Kinkaid, hailed from Cambridge's cutting-edge Harvest Restaurant, and he instantly made the restaurant the talk of the island. Among the five chefs who have followed is Michael Getter, who now owns American Seasons. It was during Getter's time at 21 Federal, in 1993, that new Culinary Institute of America graduate Russell Jaenig was hired as a line cook. Though Russell may be the youngest chef profiled in this book, he is among the most capable. This boy wonder worked his way up the ranks, taking over as executive chef in just a few years, at the age of twenty-five. Since 1996, he has further focused and refined the menu, ensuring that 21 Federal would maintain its reputation as one of the island's most consistently excellent restaurants.

Unlike Russell, Chick confides that he didn't even know where Nantucket was before he got there. In 1970, Chick and his wife, Mary, left New York City, where he had been working in advertising by day and bartending by night. He came to the island to tend bar at Gwen and Harold Gaillard's Opera House. In those days, the Opera House was *it*, a place where Nantucket's mixed community of gourmets, eccentrics, bon vivants, and salty dogs lingered late into the night. Having grown up near Carmel, California, Chick at once found that the beaches, rolling fog, and authentic charm of Nantucket agreed with his coastal sensibilities. And so did the Opera House, where he

Russell Jaehnig and Chick Walsh.

worked, first as a bartender and then as the restaurant's perfectly polished maître d'.

When Harold Gaillard passed away in 1973, Chick and Gwen established the Opera House Cup, a yearly wooden-hulled-sailboat race, in his memory. When the Opera House closed in 1986, 21 Federal took over as its unofficial headquarters.

In 1985, Chick was ready to strike out on his own. He redirected his energies to a building on Federal Street, which was then just a sleepy offshoot of bustling Main Street. The once stately home at 21 Federal completely lacked charm. It had been converted into a rooming house during the early part of the century and had housed the original Que Sera Sarah foodshop for the past two years before being put up for sale. It caught Chick's eye, and together with a group of investors, he began restoring the decaying building and converting it into a restaurant in the spring of that year.

A year later, just a week or two before opening, disaster struck. The building had been given extensive, top-to-bottom renovations, including the installation of stunning custom paneling, moldings, floors, and a gleaming cherry bar. The restaurant was staffed and set to go—only the paintings needed to be hung—when a pile of oil-soaked rags caused a devastating fire that all but burned the building to the ground. The community rallied around Chick. In an amazing outpouring of support, local painters, carpenters, electricians, and others worked overtime, many at no charge, to help Chick and his partners rebuild the restaurant, salvage the season, and open for business in time for the Fourth of July.

The restaurant has been a beloved and stately local institution ever since. Every season families, friends, businesspeople, and tourists convene at the bar or in the white-table-clothed dining rooms, keeping the atmosphere thriving and animated and the place packed. All this is exactly what Chick envisioned his restaurant to be—a convivial spot carrying on the legacy of Gwen Gaillard's Opera House, with terrific food in a welcoming milieu. So, despite the four-star talent in the kitchen, Chick doesn't want anyone to think of 21 Federal as a four-star restaurant—a place to save only for special occasions. Rather, Chick hopes that his customers will consider 21 Federal to be their "second" favorite—where the only excuse they need to come in for dinner is the desire for a terrific meal in good company.

MENU

Slow-Roasted Portobello Mushrooms with
Parmesan Pudding

Bartlett Tomatoes with Pesto Vinaigrette,
Fresh Mozzarella, Fennel, and Onion Rings

Seared Muscovy Duck Breast with
Caramelized Onion, Walnut-Cranberry
Gratin, and Fried Parsnips

Banana Bread French Toast with Bananas
Foster and Crème Fraîche

Slow-Roasted Portobello Mushrooms with Parmesan Pudding

This savory pudding has a consistency similar to a light, fluffy polenta. Use Parmigiano-Reggiano for best results.

Serves 6

6 large portobello mushrooms, wiped clean, stems removed

7 tablespoons olive oil

2 tablespoons minced garlic

¼ cup white wine

1 teaspoon salt, plus more to taste

¼ teaspoon freshly ground black pepper, plus more to taste

6 plum tomatoes

2 cups milk

1 cup heavy cream

½ cup semolina or cream of wheat

½ cup freshly grated Parmesan cheese

2 tablespoons butter

2 cups chicken stock

½ cup shredded fresh basil

Shaved Parmesan cheese, for garnish

1. Preheat the oven to 400°F. In a bowl, toss the mushrooms with 3 tablespoons of the oil. Place the caps, stem side up, on a baking sheet and spoon ½ teaspoon garlic into each cap. Fill each cap with 1 teaspoon of white wine. Sprinkle the caps with salt and plenty of black pepper.

2. In a bowl, toss the whole tomatoes with 1 tablespoon of the olive oil, 1 teaspoon of the garlic, and salt and pepper. Arrange the tomatoes on another baking sheet.

3. Bake the mushroom caps and tomatoes until the mushrooms are tender and the skins crinkle on the tomatoes, about 15 to 20 minutes (the mushrooms will be ready first). Cut each mushroom on the bias into 5 or 6 large slices. Reserve the tomatoes and any juices that may have collected on the baking sheet.

4. In a saucepan over medium-high heat, bring the milk and cream to a boil. Slowly whisk in the semolina and return to a boil briefly. Stir in the grated Parmesan, 1 teaspoon salt, and ¼ teaspoon pepper. Turn off the heat and whisk in 1 tablespoon of the butter. Cover and set aside.

5. Heat a sauté pan over medium heat before adding the remaining 3 tablespoons of oil, then add the remaining 2 teaspoons of garlic and cook until the garlic starts to turn opaque, about 1 minute. Add the sliced mushrooms and whole tomatoes with their juices, chicken stock, remaining wine, and most of the basil, reserving some basil for garnish. Bring to a boil, then lower the heat and simmer until the mixture is thick. Whisk in the remaining tablespoon of butter.

6. Spoon a portion of pudding onto each plate, arrange 5 or 6 mushroom slices around it, top with a tomato, and pour the pan sauce around the perimeter. Garnish with shaved Parmesan cheese and basil.

Bartlett Tomatoes
with Pesto Vinaigrette,
Fresh Mozzarella, Fennel,
and Onion Rings

Bartlett's Ocean View Farm supplies exquisitely flavorful tomatoes to many of the island's restaurants as well as individual residents. The superior flavor of these tomatoes is a result of Nantucket's ideal sandy soil. plus the fact that they are picked at perfect ripeness. unlike tomatoes that are picked unripe to be shipped to grocers around the country. If you are not shopping on the island. your best bet is to buy ripe tomatoes from local farm markets in the summer. Of course. if you have a garden. you can grow your own!

Serves 6 to 8

¼ cup red wine vinegar

1 tablespoon fresh lemon juice

1 teaspoon salt, plus more to taste

¼ teaspoon freshly ground black pepper, plus more to taste

1½ cups olive oil

⅓ cup grated Asiago cheese

½ cup fresh basil leaves

¼ cup pine nuts

2 garlic cloves

2 small fennel bulbs, trimmed and thinly sliced

1 tablespoon superfine sugar

1½ red onions, sliced as thin as possible

1 cup milk

1 cup all-purpose flour

1 cup cornstarch

2½ cups vegetable oil

3 large ripe tomatoes, sliced

Two 8-ounce balls of fresh buffalo mozzarella, sliced

Aged balsamic vinegar, for garnish

1. In a bowl, combine the vinegar, lemon juice, 1 teaspoon of the salt, and ¼ teaspoon of the pepper. Whisk in 1 cup of the olive oil and reserve.

2. In a food processor, process the Asiago cheese, basil, pine nuts, and garlic. Slowly pour

in the remaining ½ cup of olive oil, pulsing until the mixture is smooth; add 1 cup of the red wine vinaigrette and process to combine. Season with more salt and pepper.

3. In a bowl, combine the sliced fennel, the remaining red wine vinaigrette, and sugar. Toss to coat.

4. Soak the onion rings in the milk for a few minutes. In a wide shallow bowl, combine the flour and cornstarch. Drain the onions, discarding the milk, and dredge them in the flour mixture to coat. In a deep sauté pan or wok, heat 2½ cups vegetable oil to 350°F. Add the floured onion rings in batches and fry until golden brown, 2 to 3 minutes per batch, then transfer to a plate lined with a paper towel and season with salt and pepper.

5. On each plate, arrange the tomato slices alternating with mozzarella. Drizzle with the pesto vinaigrette and aged balsamic vinegar. Mound the fennel salad on top and arrange the onion rings along one side.

Seared Muscovy Duck Breast with Caramelized Onion, Walnut-Cranberry Gratin, and Fried Parsnips

Muscovy duck breasts are slightly leaner, and thereby meatier, than both Long Island (also called Peking) duck breasts and magret de canard, the breast from the duck used in foie gras. If muscovy drake duck breasts are not available at your butcher, you can order them by mail (see Note, page 216). If you would prefer to substitute Long Island duck breasts, cook them for a few extra minutes. If using magret de canard, note that they have a significantly larger layer of fat under the skin that needs to be rendered. To do so, cook the breasts on the fat side for about eighteen to twenty minutes, until the skin is crisp and the fat is rendered.

Russell likes to drizzle a little demi-glace over the duck before serving, but we found the dish to be nearly as excellent without it.

Serves 6

FOR THE GRATIN

1½ tablespoons vegetable oil

2 small Spanish onions, thinly sliced

1½ teaspoons salt, plus more to taste

¾ teaspoon freshly ground black pepper, plus more to taste

¼ cup white wine

3 medium Idaho potatoes, peeled and thinly sliced lengthwise

4 tablespoons (½ stick) butter, melted

1½ cups cranberries, frozen and thawed, or fresh, cleaned

½ cup chopped walnuts

FOR THE VEGETABLES

3 small beets, scrubbed and cut in quarters

2 pounds butternut squash, peeled, seeded, and cubed

1 pound parsnips, peeled, half cut into 2-inch chunks

2¼ cups olive oil

3 teaspoons minced garlic

Salt and freshly ground black pepper,
to taste

1 tablespoon butter, for finishing
vegetables

3 muscovy drake duck breasts
(1 breast will serve 2 people)

Salt and freshly ground black pepper,
to taste

1. Preheat the oven to 400°F. Butter a 9-inch loaf pan. To caramelize the onions, in a large skillet, heat the vegetable oil over high heat. Reduce the heat to medium and add the onions, 1/2 teaspoon of the salt, and 1/4 teaspoon of the pepper. Cook, stirring frequently, until the onions are deeply golden and caramelized, 15 to 20 minutes. Pour the wine into the pan, stir, and simmer until most of the liquid evaporates; set aside.

2. In a bowl, combine the potatoes, melted butter, 1 teaspoon of the salt and 1/2 teaspoon of the pepper. Assemble the gratin in the buttered loaf pan, starting with 2 layers of potatoes followed by a layer of caramelized onions and 1/2 cup of cranberries. Repeat these layers twice more. Add the walnuts to the top layer and sprinkle with salt and pepper. Cover with foil and bake for 1 hour. Remove the foil and let the nuts brown for 5 minutes. Let cool before slicing.

3. To prepare the vegetables, in a large bowl combine the beets, squash, parsnip chunks, 1/4 cup of the oil, garlic, salt, and pepper and toss well. Spread the vegetable mixture out on a baking sheet and roast for 45 minutes to 1 hour, or until slightly caramelized and tender all the way through. Let cool slightly, then remove the beet skins and chop the beets. Using a vegetable peeler, cut the remaining parsnips into thick strips.

4. To prepare the duck, score the skin of the breasts and season both sides with salt and pepper. To cook the duck and render its fat, heat a sauté pan over high heat, place the duck breasts in the pan, fat side down, lower the heat to medium-high, and cook until the fat has dripped away from the duck and the skin is crispy brown, about 10 minutes. Turn the duck breasts over and sear the flesh side over high heat for another few minutes, to brown the meat and seal in its juices. Set aside.

5. In a sauté pan over medium-high heat, heat the remaining 2 cups of oil until smoking hot and fry the parsnip strips until crispy brown, about 2 minutes. Transfer the strips to a plate lined with a paper towel.

6. When ready to serve, melt the butter in a pan over medium heat and toss the vegetables in the butter until they are reheated. Slice the duck breasts into 1/4-inch pieces and divide among the plates. Fan the duck slices around a slice of the gratin and a mound of vegetables.

Note: You can order fresh muscovy duck breasts from Joie de Vivre in Modesto, California: (800) 648-8854. On the East Coast, order from the Newark, New Jersey–based D'Artagnan, Inc.: (800) DAR-TAGN or (973) 344-0565.

Banana Bread French Toast
with Bananas Foster and
Crème Fraîche

Instead of crème fraîche, you may serve ice cream or whipped cream if you prefer.

Serves 8

FOR THE BANANA BREAD

 9 tablespoons unsalted butter, softened

1⅓ cups granulated sugar

 1 teaspoon grated orange zest

 2 large eggs

 ¼ cup honey

 6 tablespoons dry milk powder

 2 tablespoons baking powder

 ½ teaspoon vanilla extract

 ½ teaspoon salt

2⅓ cups cake flour

1¼ cups (2 to 3) mashed ripe bananas

 ½ cup chopped toasted walnuts

FOR THE BANANAS FOSTER

 4 tablespoons (½ stick) unsalted butter

 1 cup brown sugar

 ¼ cup fresh lemon juice

 4 ripe bananas, sliced

 ¼ cup crème de banane

 2 tablespoons dark rum

FOR THE FRENCH TOAST

 2 large eggs

 1 tablespoon half-and-half

 ¼ teaspoon ground cinnamon

 Butter for frying, as needed

 Crème fraîche, for garnish

 Fresh mint leaves, for garnish

1. To make the banana bread, preheat the oven to 350°F. In the bowl of an electric mixer fitted with the paddle attachment, cream the butter with the sugar and orange zest until very smooth, about 2 minutes. Add the eggs, one at a time, beating well after each addition. Beat in the honey, milk powder, baking powder, vanilla, and salt, scraping down the sides of the mixing bowl as necessary. Add the flour, beating until just combined. Stir in the bananas and nuts.

2. Scrape the batter into a greased 9-by-5-inch loaf pan and smooth the top with a spat-

ula. Bake until a tester comes out clean when inserted into the middle of the loaf, 55 to 65 minutes. If the top of the banana bread gets too brown before the middle is cooked, cover the top of the bread with a piece of foil. When the loaf is done, cool on a wire rack. Slice the banana bread into ½-inch-thick slices.

3. To make the bananas Foster, in a heavy saucepan over high heat, melt the butter. Add the brown sugar and lemon juice and bring the mixture to a boil; stir in the bananas. Carefully add the crème de banane and then the rum and continue to cook for 5 minutes longer. Cover the pan with foil to keep the mixture warm and set aside (or, reheat when ready to serve).

4. To make the French toast, in a wide shallow bowl, whisk together the eggs, half-and-half, and cinnamon. Dip the banana bread slices into the egg mixture, dredging well. Heat a sauté pan or griddle over medium heat. Add 1 tablespoon butter, lower the heat to medium-low, and melt the butter. Fry as many of the banana bread slices as will fit in one layer in the pan until they are golden brown on both sides, about 5 minutes. Transfer to a plate and tent with foil to keep warm. Continue frying the remaining slices, adding butter to the pan as necessary, until they are all done.

5. To serve, arrange 2 slices of banana bread on each plate and ladle some of the bananas Foster over them. Garnish with crème fraîche and fresh mint.

WEST CREEK CAFÉ

508-228-4943

11 WEST CREEK ROAD

SEASON: YEAR-ROUND

There's a fabulous dinner party going on outside of town, off the tourist track and away from the crowds of downtown Nantucket. It's an unpretentious affair with lively company, lots of great food and drink, and plenty of parking. Best of all, you're invited. Pat Tyler's West Creek Café is a welcoming restaurant with the feel of someone's very cozy home. But "home" includes a brilliant chef, excellent art, three distinctively quirky dining rooms, a seasonal menu that's updated weekly, and an eclectic selection of wines to choose from each evening.

This cottage at 11 West Creek Road was originally built as a private home, but in the 1970s it turned commercial along with the surrounding neighborhood, housing first the Upper Crust, and then Beach Plum Café, before Pat took over in 1995. As soon as she arrived on the scene, Pat completely renovated the place inside and out. Tiptoe through the lush flower and herb garden into the sophisticated bar area. Next is a warm and cozy room with honey-glazed walls and a splendid tangerine-crackle mantel. Finally, there is the dramatic persimmon room, whose main feature is a plush banquette lined with leopard-patterned pillows in shades of hot pink and coral.

The food at the West Creek Café, like the inviting, comfortable interior, is both appealing and approachable. Chef Jaime Hurley prepares and presents dishes that we might cook for our loved ones every night—if we had unlimited talent, time, and resources. Her menu is varied, yet refreshingly free of flash-in-the-pan trends. Instead, she focuses on bright, exuberant flavors executed with flair.

For example, salads are never mere piles of green on the plate. In Pat's restaurant, they are embellished with toasted hazelnuts and Great Hill blue cheese, olives, or other tasty tidbits. Wild mushroom risotto, a venerable dish on its own, is given both creaminess and a slight sharpness by the creative addition of a mild goat cheese. Even classic sole meunière and herb-roasted chicken receive refreshing makeovers. The fish is cornmeal-dusted, pan-fried, then paired with a spunky spinach and cheddar polenta, while the fowl is served over angel-hair pasta that's been tossed with crumbled bacon, sweet caramelized onions, and crisp green beans. While Jaime takes the lead and does the cooking during dinner service, Pat is always close at hand, tossing salads and plating desserts in the kitchen while simultaneously keeping track of everything going on in the three dining rooms.

Pat, a devoted mother of one, will be the first to tell you that she couldn't pull off the balancing act between single parenthood and restaurant management without the help of an executive chef. Luckily, she found Jaime. For her part, Jaime says that she has always felt destined to cook. She attended the Culinary Institute of America, straight out of high school. Her first externship brought her to the White Elephant on Nantucket in the summer of 1991, where she met her future husband, Lee-Jay, who also went on to become a chef on the island. Jaime started out chopping vegetables and doing other prep work for Pat in 1997, but since the start of the 1999 season she has taken creative control over the planning and preparation of the dinner menu.

You'd never guess it now, but Pat hadn't

The warm and lovely Pat Tyler.

always planned to be a restaurateur. In 1973 she was an enthusiastic home cook and well-traveled restaurant customer, but she had neither culinary education nor professional experience when she met Ben Ardrey at a dinner party and they began chatting about food. Ben offered her a cooking job at his restaurant, the Boarding House. Pat applied what she had learned from Julia Child's cookbooks, combined with her instinct to use only the freshest produce and to respect each individual ingredient. Pat eventually developed an intimate knowledge of the entire restaurant operation, and a love of the business.

After a winter stint studying cooking at La Varenne in France, Pat returned to Nantucket and spent the next three seasons as the omelet chef at Gwen Gaillard's famous

Opera House. She calls it the easiest and best job she has ever had, and it was certainly the most fun.

In 1982, full of confidence and feeling that it was time to branch out on their own, Pat and then husband David Toole opened the Second Story. The restaurant wasn't in an optimal business location, upstairs and around the corner from the downtown traffic flow. But it was there that Pat happily discovered that if your food is both exciting and reliable, customers will find you. The cuisine at Second Story was intensely creative, internationally influenced, robust, brave, and unlike anything Nantucket had seen up to that point. Pat and David utilized the spices and techniques picked up from their winters spent traveling to Portugal, Hong Kong, and Thailand. Once established, Second Story soon began to influence many of the island's chefs and restaurateurs of the time, encouraging others to reach beyond the tired repertoire of transplanted French continental food. The Second Story remained full of energy and pizzazz, and its forty-five seats were full every night they were open, from April until Christmas, for the ten years Pat was there.

In 1992, when the partnership and marriage with Toole dissolved, Pat focused her undivided attention on her son, Preston, then four years old. Once Preston was well established in grade school, Pat found herself recalling fondly the fun and frenzy of restaurant life. In short order she located a worthy space, renovated it to accommodate her own style, and opened as West Creek Café in June 1995. After twenty-five years, Pat finally had a place of her own.

MENU

Spring Pea and Sorrel Soup

■

Seared Maine Diver Scallops
with Pickled Beets, Asparagus, and Frisée

■

Grilled Pork Chops with Braised Clams,
Roasted-Garlic Mashed Potatoes,
and Oven-Roasted Haricots Verts

■

Profiteroles with Caramel Sauce

Spring Pea and Sorrel Soup

Pea shoots are the tender greens that grow from the pea plant's stalk. To prepare them, separate the green from any of the tough stem and rinse. For a low-fat version of this soup that maintains the smoothness of the original, simply omit the cream and serve it chilled. The soup will keep for two to three days tightly covered in the refrigerator.

Serves 6 to 8

1 tablespoon unsalted butter	1 tightly packed cup pea shoots, washed, plus additional for garnish
2 medium Spanish onions, chopped	
3 large celery stalks, chopped	2 tablespoons washed, dried, and chopped fresh sorrel, plus additional for garnish
4 garlic cloves, chopped	
1½ quarts water	
1 large potato, scrubbed, peeled, and chopped	1 teaspoon salt
	Freshly ground black pepper, to taste
4 cups freshly shelled and washed peas	2 cups heavy cream

1. In a sauté pan over medium heat, melt the butter. Add the onions, celery, and garlic and cook, stirring, for 3 minutes, or until tender. Add the water and potatoes and simmer for 15 minutes, or until the potatoes are tender and the onions translucent. Add the peas, pea shoots, sorrel, salt, and pepper. Simmer until the peas are just tender and still bright green, 3 to 4 minutes. Remove from the heat and let cool slightly.

2. In a blender or food processor, purée the soup in batches. Strain through a fine sieve, discarding the solids.

3. In a saucepan, bring the cream to a boil. Reduce the heat to low and whisk in the soup. Raise the heat, bring the soup back to a boil, and adjust the seasonings to taste.

4. Ladle the soup into bowls and garnish with finely shredded pea shoots and sorrel.

Seared Maine Diver Scallops with Pickled Beets, Asparagus, and Frisée

The pungent pickled beets in this recipe can be prepared up to two days in advance; leftovers make a great addition to any salad.

Serves 4

FOR THE VEGETABLES

1 large beet, well scrubbed

½ cup loosely packed light brown sugar

½ cup red wine vinegar

¼ cup rice wine vinegar

16 asparagus stalks, stems trimmed and peeled

¼ teaspoon salt

FOR THE VINAIGRETTE

Juice and grated zest of 1 washed orange

1½ tablespoons honey

¼ cup rice wine vinegar

¼ teaspoon cumin

Salt and freshly ground black pepper, to taste

½ cup olive oil

FOR THE SCALLOPS

1 tablespoon olive oil

1 tablespoon chopped shallots

Salt and freshly ground black pepper, to taste

2 bunches of frisée, washed and dried

8 large Maine diver sea scallops or regular sea scallops

Fresh chives, washed and chopped, for garnish

1. In a saucepan over high heat, boil the beet in water to cover until tender, 30 minutes to an hour depending upon the size of the beet. Drain and let cool. Peel and cut into 16 wedges.

2. In a saucepan over medium heat, combine the sugar and vinegars. Bring this mixture

WEST CREEK

CAFÉ

225

to a simmer and let cook until it is reduced by half. Turn off the heat, add the beets, and let them cool in the liquid to pickle. Reserve.

3. Fill a large bowl with ice water. Bring a large pot of water to a boil over medium-high heat. Add the asparagus and salt and cook until the asparagus are bright green and crisp-tender, about 3 minutes. Drain the asparagus, transfer them to the bowl of ice water to cool, then drain and set aside.

4. To make the vinaigrette, in a bowl, combine all of the vinaigrette ingredients except for the oil. Slowly add the oil, whisking well. Taste and adjust the seasonings if necessary.

5. To make the vegetables, in a large sauté pan, heat the oil over medium heat. Add the shallots, salt, and pepper, and sauté for 1 minute. Add the asparagus and drained beet wedges (reserve the juice) and sauté for 30 seconds. Add the frisée, stirring to wilt. Transfer the vegetables to a bowl and toss with some of the vinaigrette, to taste.

6. Heat another nonstick sauté pan over high heat until smoking hot. Place the scallops in the pan, flat side down, and sear for 1 minute; turn and sear the other side for 1 minute, until well browned. Transfer the scallops to a bowl. Pour ¼ cup of the remaining vinaigrette into the pan and swirl around to deglaze. Pour over the scallops, gently tossing to coat.

7. Mound some of the vegetables on each of 4 plates. Arrange 2 scallops over each salad, drizzle with additional vinaigrette, garnish with fresh chives, and drizzle with some of the reserved beet pickling juice.

Grilled Pork Chops with Braised Clams, Roasted-Garlic Mashed Potatoes, and Oven-Roasted Haricots Verts

Nantucket has a large population of natives descended from Portuguese fishermen (as do many southern New England port towns). This dish, with its combination of clams and pork, captures that influence.

Serves 4

FOR THE PORK CHOPS

¼ cup olive oil

1 tablespoon chopped garlic

Salt and freshly ground black pepper, to taste

Eight 4- to 5-ounce pork chops (¼ to ½ inch thick), trimmed

FOR THE MASHED POTATOES

4 Idaho potatoes, scrubbed, peeled, and cut in eighths

½ cup milk

8 garlic cloves, peeled and left whole

2 tablespoons olive oil

Salt and freshly ground black pepper, to taste

1 tablespoon unsalted butter

3 tablespoons sour cream

¼ cup light cream or half-and-half

FOR THE BEANS

Salt, to taste

1 pound haricots verts or thin green beans, trimmed

1 tablespoon olive oil

1 tablespoon unsalted butter

1 tablespoon chopped shallots

Chopped fresh chives, to taste

Freshly ground black pepper, to taste

CONTINUED

WEST CREEK

CAFÉ

227

2 tablespoons unsalted butter

1 tablespoon chopped shallots

1 teaspoon chopped garlic

4 Roma tomatoes, quartered, seeded, and finely diced

½ cup white wine

½ cup water

20 small clams, such as littlenecks, rinsed well under cold running water

1 tablespoon chopped fresh chives

Freshly ground black pepper, to taste

1. To prepare the pork chops, in a large bowl, combine the oil, garlic, and salt and pepper. Add the pork chops, turn to coat, and let marinate for up to 2 hours.

2. To make the mashed potatoes, in a pot over high heat, boil the potatoes in salted water to cover for 20 minutes, or until tender. Drain.

3. Meanwhile, preheat the oven to 350°F. In a small saucepan over high heat, bring the milk to a boil. Add the garlic cloves and return to a boil for 2 minutes. Drain the garlic cloves, rinse them, then toss with the olive oil and salt and pepper. Wrap the garlic in foil and roast for about 12 minutes, shaking every 3 minutes so the cloves don't get too dark on any one side. Let the roasted garlic cool, then coarsely chop. Keep the oven on.

4. In an electric mixer fitted with the paddle attachment, add the potatoes, garlic, butter, and sour cream and beat on low speed for 15 seconds. Scrape down the sides of the bowl, add the light cream, and beat slowly to combine, adding salt and pepper to taste. Be careful not to overbeat the potatoes or they will turn gummy. If you prefer, you can also mash the potatoes and garlic by hand.

5. To prepare the beans, fill a bowl with ice water. Bring a large pot of water to a boil. Add a large pinch of salt and the beans and cook until they are bright green and crisp-tender, about 3 minutes. Drain the beans and immediately transfer them to the ice water to stop the cooking process, then drain and set aside.

6. In an ovenproof sauté pan, add the oil and butter and place the pan in the oven until the butter melts. Add the beans, shallots, chives, and salt and pepper, tossing in the oil and butter to coat. Return to the oven for about 5 minutes, until lightly browned.

7. Raise the oven temperature to 375°F. Heat a cast-iron grill over high heat and have a baking dish standing by. Grill the marinated pork chops for 1 minute on each side to mark them, then turn 90 degrees and grill both sides again, for 1 minute each, to create a crosshatched pattern. Transfer the chops to the baking dish and bake for 5 minutes, or until done to taste (they should still be slightly pink inside).

8. For the clam sauce, heat a large sauté pan over medium heat and add 1 tablespoon of

the butter, shallots, and garlic and cook until the butter is melted. Add the tomatoes and cook until they start to break down, 2 to 3 minutes. Add the wine and water and bring the mixture to a simmer. Stir in the clams, chives, and black pepper; cover and cook for 3 to 4 minutes, or until the clams open. Discard any unopened clams. With a slotted spoon, transfer the cooked clams to a plate. Return the sauce to the stove, add the remaining tablespoon of butter, and stir until incorporated.

9. Mound a scoop of mashed potatoes on each plate. Stand two chops around the potatoes. Place 5 clams to the side and spoon sauce over the clams, making a little pool. Spoon the beans on the other side of the plate. Serve at once.

Profiteroles
with Caramel Sauce

Serves 5

FOR THE PROFITEROLES

1 cup water

4 tablespoons (½ stick) unsalted butter

1 cup all-purpose flour

4 large eggs

Vanilla ice cream, for serving

FOR THE CARAMEL SAUCE

3 cups water

1 cup sugar

3 cups heavy cream

1. To make the profiteroles, preheat the oven to 400°F. In a saucepan over medium-high heat, combine the water and butter. Bring to a boil and allow the butter to melt completely. Add the flour and stir until the mixture holds together and pulls away from the sides.

2. Immediately pour the mixture into the bowl of an electric mixer fitted with the whisk attachment. Add the eggs one at a time, pausing between additions to let the batter come back together.

3. On a parchment-lined pan, or nonstick baking sheet, place scoops of batter, about 2 heaping tablespoons each. Bake for 25 to 30 minutes, then, using a metal skewer or small knife, poke holes in each profiterole to let the air escape. Return to the oven and bake for 5 more minutes to dry. Transfer to a wire rack to cool. Split the profiteroles in half crosswise and reserve.

4. To make the caramel sauce, in a saucepan over high heat, bring the water and sugar to a rapid boil, stirring until the sugar dissolves. Stop stirring and let the mixture cook until it turns a deep amber, about 10 minutes. Turn off the heat and pour in the cream (stand back, it will splatter). Whisk the mixture over low heat until smooth. You can store the caramel sauce at room temperature for up to 2 weeks. Reheat before serving.

5. To serve, place the profiterole bottoms on plates and top with scoops of ice cream. Place the profiterole tops over the ice cream and generously drizzle with caramel sauce.

APPENDIX:
RESOURCES FOR THE
VISITOR TO NANTUCKET

GETTING THERE

Nope, there's no bridge. You'll have to arrive on Nantucket either by sea or by air. Each has its bonus. Arriving by ferry from Hyannis on Cape Cod is less expensive and more leisurely. Arriving by air is faster, and the view of Nantucket and the surrounding islands from 1,000 feet is breathtaking.

Don't plan on bringing a car on the ferry unless your visit is for a month or longer. The cost is prohibitive by design because there are too many vehicles on Nantucket already. Instead, rent one that's already there, bring your bicycle on the ferry or rent one for use on the island's wonderful bike paths, or make use of the Nantucket Regional Transit Authority (NRTA) public shuttle, and augment with taxis. Most of the restaurants featured are within walking distance of town and one another.

As a popular bumper sticker on the island says, FOG HAPPENS. It's never a good idea to cut your travel plans to Nantucket too close. You never know when the airport might shut down for a few hours until visibility improves, or high winds might slow down the ferry schedule. Be as flexible as possible and you might be rewarded with an extra day or two to enjoy all that the island has to offer.

FERRIES

STEAMSHIP AUTHORITY
South Street Dock, Hyannis, Mass.
Car ferry information and reservations:
508-477-8600
Operates year-round. No reservation required for passengers, bicycles, and pets. Parking available for a fee in Hyannis. Takes approximately two hours.

FAST FERRY
508-495-FAST
Reservations recommended. No vehicles or pets, and limited bicycle space for a fee. Takes approximately one hour.

HY-LINE CRUISES
Ocean Street Dock, Hyannis, Mass.
508-778-2600
Offers a variety of year-round and seasonal options, including a high-speed catamaran and service to Martha's Vineyard.

LOCAL AIRLINES

NANTUCKET AIRLINES
800-635-8787
Thirteen-minute flights available hourly, year-round, from Hyannis on Cape Cod. Airport parking available.

CAPE AIR
800-325-0714
Flights available from Boston; Martha's Vineyard; New Bedford, Mass.; and Providence, R.I.

Those driving from the New York area might prefer a longer flight from New Bedford or Providence with less driving time than to Hyannis. Parking available at all airports.

ISLAND AIRLINES
800-248-7779 or 508-228-7575
Also services the island hourly, year-round from Hyannis.

MAJOR AIRLINES
Most national airlines can make connections with Cape Air in either Boston or Providence.

USAIR EXPRESS
800-428-4322
Service from Boston and La Guardia, N.Y.

CONTINENTAL EXPRESS
800-525-0280
Seasonal service from Newark, N.J.

AMERICAN EAGLE
800-433-7300
Seasonal service from Boston.

BY PRIVATE PLANE

AIRPORT OPERATIONS
508-325-5307

BY PRIVATE BOAT

NANTUCKET BOAT BASIN
800-NAN-BOAT

NANTUCKET MOORINGS
508-228-7260

TOWN PIER
508-228-7260

BUS SERVICE TO HYANNIS

BONANZA BUS LINE
from New York City: 212-947-1766
from Providence: 800-556-3815

PLYMOUTH AND BROCKTON BUS LINE
508-778-9767
Service from Boston and Logan Airport.

USEFUL SOURCES OF INFORMATION

www.nantucket.net
An online overview of the island with links to lodging, restaurant, retail, and real-estate sites as well as information on weather and transportation.

www.nantucketdirectory.com
Nantucket's newest phone book is conveniently online. Let your fingers do the walking.

VISITOR'S SERVICES
508-228-0925
Located downtown on Federal Street, they distribute maps and information for the island's many visitors and can assist you with last-minute accommodations. Public bathrooms and a bank of pay phones are also conveniently located there.

NANTUCKET ISLAND CHAMBER OF COMMERCE
508-228-1700; www.nantucketchamber.org
There's not much the good folks at the NICC can't help you with. They publish a terrific visitor's guide with information and detailed maps on transportation and schedules, activities for the family, beaches, cultural and historical sites, special events, accommodations, arts and antiques, food and dining, real estate, sports and recreation—you name it. The guide is published yearly and is available by phone or through their website.

LODGING

NANTUCKET LODGING ASSOCIATION
www.nantucketlodging.org
Nantucket is home to literally hundreds of lovely places to stay, from the smallest, quaint little inn to a larger, luxury hotel. Almost all are members of this association and are linked through their website. In keeping with the island-wide ban on "chain" businesses, don't expect to find any Sheratons or Holiday Inns. Due to the island's fragile ecology, camping is also prohibited.

NANTUCKET ACCOMMODATIONS
508-228-9559
This for-profit organization can help make a good fit between your needs and the island's many lodging options. They take their cut from the inns they service, so it's at no additional cost to you. They also keep a frequently updated list on hand of last-minute availability and cancellations and can help you find a bed in a pinch.

NANTUCKET ISLAND RESORTS
800-ISLANDS
Owners of the Wauwinet (Topper's), White Elephant (Brant Point Grill), Harbor House (Food Fare), Boat Basin, and Wharf Cottages. They have many options for accommodations at a range of prices and can offer a level of service that exceeds that of the average inn or bed and breakfast. If you're looking for a full-service hotel, stick with an NIR property. The newly refurbished White Elephant and Brant Point Grill is right on the harbor, in town, and stunning.

FOR A TASTE OF NANTUCKET HISTORY

THE NANTUCKET HISTORICAL ASSOCIATION
508-228-1894
Founded in 1894 to help preserve Nantucket's unique and fascinating history. They manage many fantastic museums and properties, including the Whaling Museum and the Oldest House. If history is your thing, all-inclusive passes to NHA sites are available and recommended.

THE NANTUCKET ATHENAEUM
508-228-1110
The library, to you and me. It is one of the oldest in the United States and is located in a stunning 1847 Greek Revival building in the heart of downtown on India Street. Included in their 40,000-some volumes is just about every book and guide ever written about Nantucket.

GOURMET SHOPPING

BARTLETT'S OCEAN VIEW FARM
508-228-9403;
www.bartlettsoceanviewfarm.com
If you can't make it out of town, Bartlett's farm truck is parked on Main Street all season long. If you can, take a left off the Hooper Farm Road on your way to Cisco Beach for a visit to foodie paradise. The people at Bartlett's invite you to "take a vacation from your kitchen" with a terrific assortment of prepared foods, gourmet pastas, sauces, and condiments. During peak season, you almost don't need to go anywhere else to do your food shopping, except maybe to a local fishmonger, and there's a great one right down the street.

EAST COAST SEAFOOD
167 Hummock Pond Road
508-228-2871
Proprietor Bill Sandole supplied only local

restaurants for many years before opening his retail operation in 1997. The first thing you'll notice is how clean it is. The fish and seafood is always the very freshest and of the best quality available. Call ahead with your order and they'll have it ready for you.

CISCO BREWERY
5 Bartlett Farm Road
508-325-5929
Just before Bartlett's on the left is Nantucket's one and only local brewery. Lucky for us, the beer that they produce year-round in small batches, the old-fashioned way, is top-notch. Call for hours or just stop by on your way to the farm.

NANTUCKET VINEYARDS
5 Bartlett Farm Road
508-228-9235
The same property as Cisco Brewery is home to Nantucket's only local winery. Produced primarily from Washington State grapes, a riesling, sauvignon blanc, merlot, zinfandel, and their Sailor's Delight, a light blended red, are available to taste and take home year-round.

DAMIANO'S MARKET
14 Amelia Drive
508-228-5879
This gourmet meat market also offers fresh pasta and produce. Call for hours of operation, year-round.

NANTUCKET GOURMET
4 India Street
508-228-4353
Home to exotic ingredients, tools, appliances, some cheeses and prepared foods, cookbooks, and even great sandwiches to go.

THE COMPLETE KITCHEN
25 Centre Street
508-228-2665
Nantucket is blessed with not one, but two great kitchen shops and they are just around the corner from each other. The Complete Kitchen has more tabletop offerings, and a large freezer with prepared hors d'oeuvres and pastas for convenient entertaining.

FAHEY & FROMAGERIE
49-A Pleasant Street
508-325-5644
The Fahey part of the name is Michael Fahey, former wine steward at Topper's. He specializes in lesser-known and hard-to-find wine, primarily French, and is usually on hand with suggestions and cheese pairings. The cheese selection is superb, as are the prepared foods and desserts. Don't resist sweet offerings from pastry chef Jodi Levesque, who also supplies several of the island's best restaurants with desserts.

ACK NATURAL
95 Washington Street Extension
508-228-4554
This charming shop on the edge of town and across the street from the harbor features or-

ganic meats, poultry, produce, a full line of whole-food groceries, vitamins and supplements, and fresh-squeezed juices and smoothies.

NANTUCKET NATURAL

Meeting House Shops at 29 Centre Street
508-228-3947
This in-town health food store offers a full assortment of whole foods, terrific smoothies, teas, vitamins, homeopathic medicines, natural beauty products, and good solid advice.

NANTUCKET WINE FESTIVAL

www.nantucketwinefestival.com
Now several years old and well established, the Nantucket Wine Festival, held each spring, is not to be missed. Denis Toner, former wine steward at the Chanticleer, organizes several days of grand tastings, intimate wine-maker dinners, and vertical tastings in breathtaking private homes. Check the website for dates and additional information.

THE FIRE HOUSE

4 East Chestnut Street
508-228-0184
Nantucket's only source for fine cigars, pipe tobacco, and new and antique smoking accessories. A large walk-in humidor is always well stocked with the best major brands and a few lesser-known surprises. Proprietor Mark Mormar is a great source of information and good company. I should know; he's my husband!

OTHER GOOD EATING

In addition to the restaurants featured in this book, there are dozens more great spots to visit for everything from French fries by the coneful and chicken burritos to the finest chateaubriand. Don't miss lower Broad Street on Steamboat Wharf for greasy burgers, fried clams, and pizza, among other "I-need-a-break-from-fine-dining" delights. The Lobster Trap is a favorite of many families, and if you want to eat like an islander, the Sea Grill is the place for you. As for fine dining, 56 Union, the Woodbox, India House, the Summer House, Brant Point Grill at the new White Elephant Hotel, the Rope Walk, the Centre Street Bistro, and the brand-new Sfoglia are all worthy of a visit.

Though there always seems to be a shortage of restaurants that are open for lunch, Cioppino's, the Galley on Cliffside Beach, the Tap Room, the Brotherhood, the Summer House Pool during season, and the Brant Point Grill are all a good bet. Breakfast is one of our favorite meals to eat out on Nantucket, and no one does it better than the Downeyflake. Try their fresh-made chocolate glazed doughnuts and eggs every way from scrambled to Benedict.

INDEX

ABOUT THE AUTHORS

MELISSA CLARK writes about cuisine and is a regular contributor to *The New York Times*, among other publications. A former professional caterer, she earned an M.F.A. in writing from Columbia University and began a freelance food-journalism career in 1993. She is the author of eleven cookbooks. Clark lives in Brooklyn, New York, with her family.

SAMARA FARBER MORMAR began her Nantucket culinary career at the Boarding House restaurant. After several seasons in the kitchens of the Club Car and Straight Wharf, she returned to her original home of New York, where she was a cook at the Russian Tea Room, an executive chef for a prominent New York catering company, and, for four years, a restaurant publicist. She currently lives on Nantucket year-round with her husband, Mark, and son, Max, and their three dogs.